NATIONAL MUSEUM

CLIO EDITIONS

athens 1993

ISBN. 960-7465-02-4

Art layout: RACHEL MISDRACHE-CAPON

Photographs: M. SKIADARESES, N. KONTOS, S. TSAVDAROGLOU

Colour separation: "EUROGRAPH"

BASIL PETRAKOS: Ephor of Antiquities in Attica

NATIONAL MUSEUM

SCULPTURE - BRONZES - VASES

History of the foundation of the National Archaeological Museum

The particular importance of Greece's museums as compared with most ancient Greek art collections in the museums of other countries resides in the fact that the antiquities kept in the former are largely original works of art, most of them found at scientifically conducted excavations, so that we know both the place to which they belonged and their significance for that place. E.g. the tomb relief No 833, which we will see in the room of Aristonautes, is not merely a grave decoration or just a work commissioned to a sculptor's workshop, but is associated with the people who ordered it and with those who, in their ideal forms, are represented in it. The persons in relief 833 are well known and so is their great and numerous family. We know where they were born and where they lived, we have found their tomb, and we can walk along the same footpaths and roads they trod some 2300 years ago. One can tell a little story about nearly every one of the exhibits in Greek museums. In contrast, many of the famous works kept in foreign museums are either copies produced by the "art industry" of the Roman period to adorn the mansions and palaces of rich nobles or are indeed important originals but found under unknown or uncertain and undocumented circumstances.

The National Archaeological Museum of Athens, as it is now officially known, concentrates in its display-halls and store-rooms the most splendid works of ancient art found in Greece. Under the regulations in force in the past century, all important archaeological finds went to the National Museum; exceptions were made only for some of the greatest centres of Ancient Greece, such as Delphi, Olympia and Crete.

When local museums were created later, these regulations were abolished and new finds are now kept at the site of discovery or in the nearest museum.

Almost as soon as the free Greek state came into being, the Greeks decided to create a central museum. The first archaeological museum was set up in the premises of the then orphanage (now prison) of Aegina in 1829. A few years later, in 1837, most, and the best, of the exhibits were moved to Athens and settled in the Theseion.

While the central museum was at Aegina, archaeological discoveries resulting either from excavations or from accidental finds in Athens itself were collected in

the church known as Megali Panagia. In 1835, these were moved to the Theseion, the ancient temple of Hephaestos, which had been turned into the "Central Archaeological Museum" by a royal decree of 1834. The Theseion, however, was not large enough to accommodate the ever-increasing number of finds, and many had to be stored in Hadrian's Library, the Tower of the Winds. Alongside these governmental activities, the Archaeological Society, a private association operating under government supervision, had set up its own museum at the University. Removed from the University in 1863, that museum was first attached to the Varvakeion Lyceum in 1865 and later moved to the Polytechnio.

The donation of a large plot in Patission st. by Eleni Tositsa, and a generous initial cash grant by Dimitrios Bernardakis, permitted the erection of the present building of the National Archaeological Museum to be started. Actual construction lasted from 1860 to 1889. The original design by L. Lange was subsequently modified and completed by E. Ziller. Further additions and changes made before and after World War II, have resulted in the present form of the Museum.

The present arrangement of the exhibits dates from the period after World War II and is due for the most part to the great Greek archaeologist and then curator of the museum Christos Carousos, his wife Semni Carousou, and their co-workers.

Chronological synopsis

In order to understand a work of art, some knowledge of the period in which it was created and of the people then living is essential. This is particularly true of Ancient Greece, where artistic creations were not meant as mere embellishments of the life of the Greeks but as ordinary necessities. The statues, the steles, the temples, were made by people who felt a need for these things in their everyday lives. They lived in a time of great events: wars, colonisations, struggles. While sculptors, painters and craftsmen created the works we are going to see, philosophers, poets and historians used a different medium — the word — to express the thoughts and feelings of the Greeks. All of these elements — art, philosophy, poetry, history — must be considered together if one is to really understand the unity of all the creations of the spirit. The following concise chronological table will help locate the main historical and spiritual events that occurred in the Greek world.

B.C.

6100-2800	Neolithic Age	**abt. 624**	Draco's laws in Athens.
3200-1100	Aegean civilization	**abt. 600**	*Arion in the Court of Periandros in Corinth.* Foundation of Marseille.
2300-1900	Early Hellenic period		
1900-1600	Middle Hellenic period	**600-595**	*Sappho's prime.*
1600-1100	Mycenaean civilization	**594/3**	Solon's term of office as archon of Athens.
1000-900	Early geometric age	**590**	*Temple of Hera at Olympia.*
900-700	Geometric age - *Homeric poems.*	**561/60**	Peisistratos tyrant of Athens.
776	First Olympic games: Coroibos of Elia stadium race winner.	**556-468**	*The poet Simonides of Kea.*
754	Beginning of the list of ephores in Sparta.	**536/5-533/2**	*Thespis stages the first tragedy at the great Dionysian games.*
middle 8th c.	Second colonization period: foundation of Kyme in Campania, of Sinope and Trebizond in Pontos.	**529-519**	*Peisistratos' temple on Athena of the Acropolis.*
		528/27	Death of Peisistratos; rule of his sons Hippias and Hipparchos.
late 8th c.	First Messenian war		
abt. 700	*Hesiod, Archilochos, Tyrtaeos.* Foundation of Taras.	**525/24**	*Birth of Aeschylus.*
		518-438	*The poet Pindar.*
abt. 688	Foundation of Gela.	**515-510**	*Construction of the temple of Olympian Zeus in Athens.*
1st half 7th c.	Lelantian war.		
676-673	*Musical victory of Terpandros in Sparta.*	**514**	Assassination of Hipparchos by Aristogeiton at the Great Panathenian Games.
abt. 650	Tyranny in Greece; Kypselos tyrant of Corinth	**510**	Overthrow of Hippias in Athens.
middle 7th c.	Second Messenian war.		
abt. 640	*Birth of Solon.*	**508/7**	Political reforms of Cleisthenes in Athens.
632	Kylon's rebellion in Athens.	**506**	The Athenians defeat the Boeotians and the Chalkideans.
abt. 630	Foundation of Kyrene.		
630/20	*Birth of the poet Alkaeos.*	**497/96**	*Birth of Sophocles.*

abt. 495/86	Temple of Aphaea at Aegina.	456	Death of Aeschylus.
493	Themistocles becomes archon of Athens.	454	Transfer of the treasury of the Athenian Alliance from Delos to Athens.
490	Campaign of Datis and Artaphernes against Eretria and Athens; destruction of Eretria; battle of Marathon.	450-425	Temple of Apollo at Bassae in Arcadia.
		449	Peace of Kallias.
488/80	Earlier Parthenon built on the Acropolis of Athens.	449-444	Temple of Hephaestos in Athens.
480	Battle of Thermopylae, sea-battle of Artemission, sea-battle of Salamis.	447-432	The Parthenon built on the Acropolis of Athens.
479	Battle of Plataeae and Mycale; Athens fortified with walls.	446-45	Thirty-year truce between Athens and Sparta.
478/77	First Athenian Alliance.	abt. 445	Birth of Aristophanes; birth of Lysias.
476	"Phoenicians" of Phrynichos.		
472	"Persians" of Aeschylus.	444/3	Establishment of Thouria.
471	Ostracism of Themistocles.	444-440	Temple of Poseidon at Sounion in Attica.
470	Birth of Socrates.	442	Sophocles' "Antigone".
468-60	Temple of Zeus at Olympia.	438	Euripides' "Alcestis".
467	"Seven against Thebes" of Aeschylus.	437-432	The Propylaea built on the Acropolis of Athens.
464	Third Messenian war.	436	Birth of the orator Isocrates.
460	Birth of the historian Thucydides.	436-432	Temple of Nemesis at Ramnous, Attica.
460-450	"Ajax" of Sophocles.	432	Resolution of Megara.
460	Athenian campaign in Egypt.	431	Euripides' "Medea".
abt. 460	Birth of Hippocrates at Cos.	431-404	Peloponnesian War.
458	Aeschylus' "Oresteia".	430	Epidemic in Athens. Birth of Xenophon, the historian.

429	Death of Pericles.
428	Birth of Plato. Euripides' "Hippolytus.
427-424	Temple of Athena - Nike on the Acropolis of Athens.
425	Landing of the Athenian general Demosthenes at Pylos; capture of Spartan hoplites at Sphacteria. Aristophanes' "Acharneans".
424	Defeat of the Athenians at Delion.
423	Aristophanes' "Clouds."
422	Death of Cleon and Vrassidas at Amphipolis.
421	Aristophanes' "Peace."
421-414	Peace between Athens and Sparta.
421-405	The Erechtheion built on the Acropolis of Athens.
415	Campaign of the Athenians in Sicily. Euripides' "Trojans".
414	Resumption of the war between Athens and Sparta.
411	Dictatorship of the 400 in Athens.
409	Sophocles' "Philoctetes".
408	Euripides' "Orestes".
406	Sea-battle of Arginoussae.
405	Sea-battle of Aigos Potamoi. Aristophanes' "Frogs".
404	Fall of Athens. The Thirty Tyrants.
401	Campaign of Cyrus and the 10,000. Sophocles' "Oedipus at Colonos".
399	Death of Socrates.

392	Aristophanes' "Ecclessiazoussae".
388	Aristophanes' "Ploutos".
384	Birth of Aristotle; birth of Demosthenes.
380	Isocrates' "Panegyricus".
abt. 380	Temple of Asklepios at Epidaurus.
371-362	Theban hegemony.
abt. 374	Plato's "Republic".
368/7	Aristotle in Athens.
349	First "Philippic" of Demosthenes.
349/48	Three "Olynthic" orations of Demosthenes.
348/7	Death of Plato.
343/2	Aristotle appointed tutor to Alexander the Great; birth of Menandros.
341	Birth of Epicurus; third and fourth "Philippics" of Demosthenes.
339	The "Panathenian" oration by Isocrates.
338	Battle of Cheroneia. Death of Isocrates.
336	Assassination of Philip II of Macedon.
335	Destruction of Thebes by Alexander.
335/4	Return of Aristotle to Athens.
334	Alexander's campaign against the Persians.
333/32	Birth of Zenon, founder of the "Stoa".
323	Death of Alexander the Great (10th June).

322	Death of Aristotle; Demosthenes commits suicide.	183	Death of Philopoimen, the leader of the Achaean commonwealth.
319	Sponsor's monument of Nikias in Athens.	171-168	The Romans start war against Perseus, king of Macedon.
317-307	Demetrios of Phaleron becomes ruler of Athens.	168	Battle of Pydna, defeat of Perseus.
316	Menandros' "Dyscolos".	148	Macedonia becomes a Roman province.
312/11	Zeno's arrival in Athens.		
late 4th c.	Birth of the poet Callimachos at Kyrene.	146	Destruction of Corinth by the Roman Consul Mommius.
301	Battle of Ipso; death of Antigonus the One-Eyed. Zeno founds the "Stoa".	31	Sea-battle of Aktion.
		30	Fall of Alexandria; death of queen Cleopatra.
300-200	The poet Theocritus.	27	Greece becomes a Roman province
295-290	Birth of the poet Apollonius of Rhodes.		
291/0	Death of Menandros.		
287-212	Archimedes, the great mathematician from Syracuse.	**A.D.**	
270	Death of the philosopher Epicurus.	middle 1st c.	Birth of the philosopher Epictetus.
263	Foundation of the Kingdom of Pergamus.	abt. 46	Birth of the historian and philosopher Plutarch.
		117-138	Emperor Hadrian.
246/45	Callimachos writes the poem "The Lock of Berenice" in Alexandria.	abt. 120	Birth of Lucian.
		124/5	Emperor Hadrian in Athens.
abt. 240	Death of Callimachos.	abt. 126	Death of Plutarch.
222	Battle of Sellasia; occupation of Sparta by the Macedonians.	128/9+131/2	Emperor Hadrian in Athens.
214-129	The philosopher Carneadis.	abt. 150	Pausanias tours Greece.
abt. 200	Birth of the historian Polyvius at Megalopolis.	161-180	Emperor Marcus Aurelius.
		205-270	The philosopher Plotinus.
abt. 110	Death of Polyvius.	391	Destruction of the Serapeion of Alexandria.
197	Battle of Kynos Kephalai; defeat of the Macedonians by the Roman Consul Flamininus.	393	Last (293rd) Olympic Games.

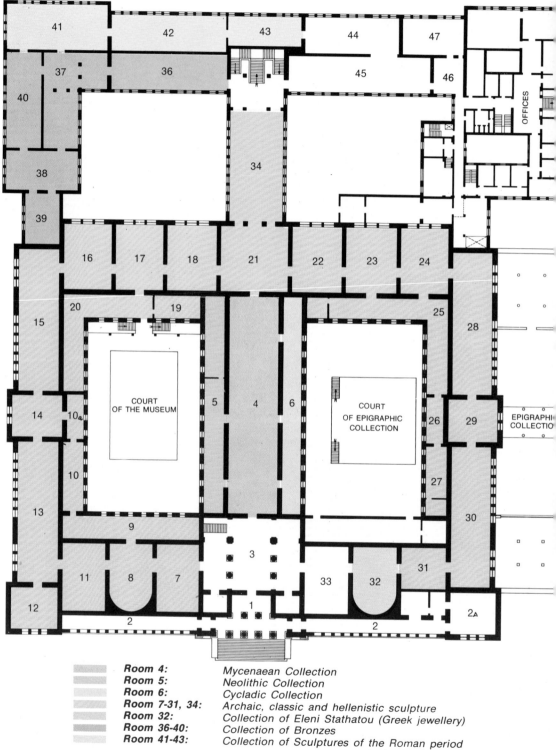

Room 4:   Mycenaean Collection
Room 5:   Neolithic Collection
Room 6:   Cycladic Collection
Room 7-31, 34:   Archaic, classic and hellenistic sculpture
Room 32:   Collection of Eleni Stathatou (Greek jewellery)
Room 36-40:   Collection of Bronzes
Room 41-43:   Collection of Sculptures of the Roman period

(redrawing by John Travlos)

PREHISTORIC COLLECTIONS

The so-called "prehistoric" period of the Greek area is represented by an unbelievable wealth and a unique variety of finds in the first three rooms of the National Museum immediately adjacent to the large entrance hall, and on the first floor, where finds from Thera are exhibited. The prehistoric objects shown in the Museum are mainly the result of two great and systematic excavations and they are displayed in such a way as to provide an overall picture of the period in which they were created.

Room 5. Neolithic Age Collection

Displayed in the long and narrow room to the left of the central room housing the Mycenaean collection are mainly relics of the Neolithic Age from Sesklon, Dimini, and other parts of Thessaly, and from Phthiotis, Boeotia, Locris, Lemnos, Attica and Troy.

The exploration of the Neolithic Age in Thessaly, represented here by a large number and variety of finds, was instituted by the Greek archaeologist Christos Tsountas, who also determined its chronological limits. Subsequent investigators have extended research to earlier stages of the Neolithic Age civilisation and have modified considerably the general chronological framework defined by Tsountas, though without essentially changing his basic conclusions.

In the characteristic words of D.R. Theocharis, one of Tsountas's successors in the exploration of neolithic Thessaly, "theoretically at least, the back of "historical" events and persons, precludes the setting of any absolute date in prehistory". This should be borne in mind as one views the prehistoric collections in the Museum. Nonetheless, scientific experts have been able to arrive at certain generally accepted conclusions with regard to the dates of the neolithic period in the prehistory of the Greek area. The following table summarises the prevailing views:

6100-5800	Pre-ceramic neolithic age
5800-4300	Early neolithic age
4300/200 - 2800/700	Late neolithic age

In classical civilisations, especially that of Greece, archaeological finds are one of our sources of information about the people of the period concerned and their history; a second source consists of the writings of historians, poets, philosophers and other writers, many of which have been preserved. In respect of prehistoric ages, on the other hand, and that is particularly true of the New Stone or neolithic Age, we only have monuments - including movable objects and buildings - to tell us about the people, their ways of life and their beliefs. Thus prehistoric finds are valuable and indeed irreplaceable witnesses of prehistoric civilisations and sole sources of information about them.

The term *Neolithic Age* does not denote any abrupt turning point in human civilisation; it is rather a conventional term as are all separations of the history of mankind into broad periods of time.

Show-case 34: Early neolithic ceramic and stone axes from Sesklon.

Show-case 35: Sesklon, early neolithic age: of special interest is the

*1. Vase with colour decoration No 5925, from Sesklo. **2a.** Spherical vase No 5922 with two-colour decoration,from Dimini. **2b.** Spherical vase No 8051 from Lianokladi.*

bowl-shaped, colour-decorated vase No **5925** and the four-sided utensil No **6036.**

Base 5894: Uncommonly interesting for its shape and size is the ithyphallic clay figurine of a male divinity of the later neolithic from the region of Larissa.

Show-case 36: Clay figurines from Sesklon: of particular interest are those representing an obese female deity. No **5937:** clay figurine, 0,16 m high, of a "kourotrophos", i.e. of a woman holding a baby in her arms, of the late neolithic age. This kind of figurine occurs again in subsequent periods and often has a religious significance.

Show-case 37: Clay and stone figurines from the Acropolis of Dimini.

Show-case 49: From the Acropolis of Dimini: No **5922,** exquisite, near-spherical, red-and-black clay vase with two handles and upright cylindrical rim, decorated with overlapping stripes, lines, spirals, broken lines; dated to the late neolithic age. No **5929,** small, 0,085 m high vase with two handles, rounded part decorated with engraved designs. No **5994,** marble figurine of the late neolithic age, showing a highly schematised human figure.

Show-case 39: This show-case contains clay objects illustrating the various stages of Thessalian ceramic art from the neolithic to the bronze age.

Show-case 40: Ceramics from Orchomenos in Boeotia and Lianocladi in Phthiotis. An excellent specimen is vase No **8051** with its spherical shape and its simple though marked and coloured "scraped" decoration enhancing the beauty of the shape.

Show-case 46: Vases from the early and mid-Helladic settlement of

3
3. *Gold jewellery No 7159 from Poliochni, Lemmos.* 4. *Figurine No 5894 showing seated man, from Thessaly.* 5. *Figurine of a woman holding a child No 5937, from Sesklo.*

Orchomenos in Boeotia, and pre-Mycenaean and Mycenaean vases from the same location.

Show-cases 43 and 45: Finds from Nea Macri and Raphina of Attica. Of special importance for the early history of Attica are the finds from the neolithic settlement of Nea Macri on the coast of Attica near Marathon. Later excavations at Nea Macri itself and at nearby Ramnous on the Euboic Gulf have uncovered evidence of busy activity in the region during the neolithic age. *Ceramics from the early Helladic settlement of Raphina.* Raphina is the origin of the fine vases in show-case 45. Note in particular the lovely shape of the "sauce-container" No **8858** and the pitcher No **8863.**

Show-case 41: Finds from the excavation of Poliochne at Lemnos. The excavations were carried out by the Italian School of Archaeology and all of the four successive neolithic settlements (2700-2000 B.C.) discovered - they were inhabited by populations related to those of Asia Minor - have yielded pottery, tools and weapons made of bronze, and gold jewellery like the gold-earrings No **7159.**

Show-case 42: Pottery of the mid-Helladic period from Aphidnae in Attica. Early Helladic and Mycenaean pottery, marble figurines and pan-shaped utensils (mirrors), reminiscent of similar finds of Cycladic style found in graves and houses in the corresponding settlements of Agios Kosmas on the coast of Attica.

Show-case 44: Pottery, figurines and jewellery from the successive settlements of Troy excavated by H. Schliemann.

Room 6. Cycladic Collection

The islands of the Aegean Sea, named Cyclades by the ancients because they form an approximate circle around Delos, the island sacred to Apollo, are part of the Archipelago. The main islands are about 20 in number, but there is a multitude of smaller and uninhabited ones. Being isolated from the Greek mainland by the sea, though many of them form a continuation of continental Greece (Andros, Tinos, Myconos and Delos are a projection of Euboea while Makronisos, Kea, Kythnos, Seriphos and Siphnos are a projection of Attica), they developed in prehistoric times a distinct civilisation of their own, described by the early investigator of that civilisation Christos Tsountas as Cycladic, from the collective name of the islands involved.

The development of the Cycladic civilisation paralleled that of the Greek mainland and of Crete. Its various periods are dated as follows:

Early Cycladic civilisation
1st stage	**3200-2800 B.C.**
2nd stage	**2800-2300 B.C.**
3rd stage	**2300-2000 B.C.**
Middle Cycladic civilisation	**2000-1600 B.C.**
Late Cycladic civilisation	**1600-1100 B.C.**

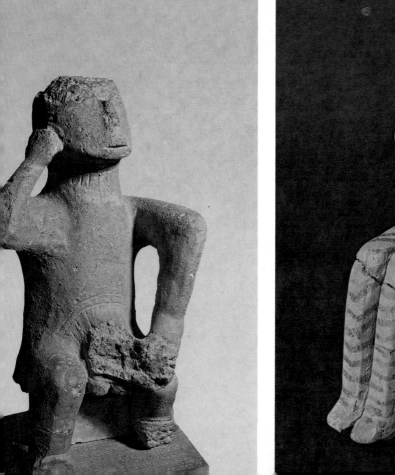

6. Cycladic figurine of a harp-player No 3908, from Keros. 7. Cycladic figurine of a flute-player No 3910, from Keros. 8. Large Cycladic figurine of a standing nude woman No 3978, from Amorgos.

3978. Intact, 1,52 m high statue from Amorgos, representing a goddess standing on tip-toe like a dancer. The hands are folded below the breasts and, as is customary in Cycladic figurines, the left arm is always over the right arm. The breasts are very high and the neck is elongated as is the entire body and the head with the broad forehead and nose. The other facial features were painted on, a practice also prevalent in other periods. This is the largest statue preserved from the Cycladic age.

3909. This life-size head of a statue of a goddess, comes from Amorgos. The mouth and the ears are moulded in addition to the nose in this case. Traces of paint indicate that other details of the head were again painted on.

3910. A precursor of the splendid flute-players of the classical era, this statuette from Keros represents a standing man playing the double flute which he is holding in his hands; with its feet firmly stepping on the contiguous base, the full body has aliveness and movement.

3908. Coming from Keros, this small statue shows a male figure seated on a throne and playing a triangular musical instrument (harp). This bold composition with the composite movement and the "abstraction" of which the sculptor seems capable, is a true work of art, a masterpiece of Cycladic sculpture.

Show-case 52: Objects found in "Cycladic" graves of Naxos; particularly noteworthy are the pyxis No **5358** with its lid whose entire surface is covered with raised spirals, the series of figurines representing a female goddess (No **6140**), the tools used in wood and stone work, a.o.

Show-case 54: Finds from a grave of Naxos: the most significant include the pan-shaped clay utensil No **6140A,** which is decorated with engraved spirals and fishes, the five marble figurines under the general number **6140;** the latter, however, are inferior in anatomical rendering, esp. of the extremities, compared with the goddess **3978** and the musicians **3908** and **3910.**

Show-cases 56 and 57: The so-called frying pans displayed here come from graves excavated at Chalantriani of Syros by Christos Tsountas and are noted for their unusual form: the outer surface is flat and decorated with geometric designs or pictorial representations; these include small ships, while No **6140** is engraved with four fishes and as many spirals. According to Tsountas's interpretation, these utensils served as mirrors when the concave inner surface, which is smooth and free of decorations, was filled with water. Other interpretations ascribe to these objects a metaphysical, religious or even magical significance, while the various interpretations of the decoration seem to reflect the views of the investigators rather than those of the people who made the objects for their own use or pleasure. In many of these utensils there is, above the handle, an indication of the pubic triangle seen in marble female figurines; this is regarded as strong evidence in favour of the mirror theory.

Phylacopi of Melos: Lying SW of the other Cyclades, Melos at one time acquired considerable significance, owing mainly to two factors: one was its geographical position on the sea route between Crete and the Peloponnese, esp. Argolis, the centre of Mycenaean Civilisation, the other was its vast reserves of the hard, shining black rock known as obsidian. As a result of these factors, Melos developed a brisk trade, grew into a flourishing community, and produced excellent works of pottery and painting under the double influence of vases imported from

9. Marble figurine of the earlier neolithic No 3928, from Sparta.
10. Cycladic figurine of a nude woman No 6174, from Syros.

both Crete and Greece proper. In the earlier period, i.e. toward the end of the 3rd millennium, the dominant influence seems to have been Cretan, as Cretans settled down on the island and established a trading post at Phylacopi, a fortified coastal town serving as a port; later, around 1600, the Mycenaean influence prevailed in the art of both Melos and the other Cyclades.

Excavations conducted by the English Archaeological School at Phylacopi brought to light three successive settlements (Phylacopi I, II, III), from which the striking exhibits at the far end of the room were recovered. The vases differ from those encountered elsewhere in shape, decoration techniques (e.g. use of red within a black outline) as well as subjects, which are floral (lilies, saffron, reed) or animal (humans, fish, birds).

Show-case 66, Phylacopi. **5782:** cylindrical clay base of a vase, with a circular representation of fishermen - men wearing only a loin-cloth and walking to the right, carrying a fish in each hand; the contour of each figure is indicated by a black line, while the interior is brown; despite its artlessness, the design reveals a sense of painting.

On the wall: Frescoes of Phylacopi. **5844,** fragments of a fresco showing flying fish with an uncommonly vivid sense of movement.

11

12

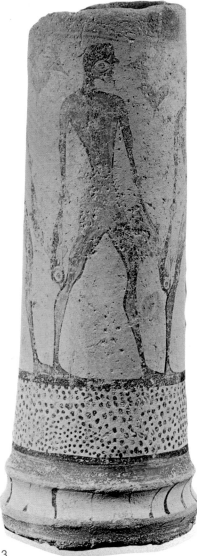

13

Room 4. Mycenaean Collection

As Orestes, the son of Agamemnon arrived at Mycenae in the tragedy "Electra" of Sophocles, his tutor pointed to the city saying: Here we are in gold-rich Mycenae. To Sophocles who lived in the 5th century B.C., this attribute of Mycenae was only of historical significance, but it was a designation of very ancient origin, known to Homer at a time when the legendary wealth of the Mycenaeans was a living memory among the ancients.

The tragic fate of the kings of Mycenae, and the awe-inspiring ruins of the city, were some of the incentives that induced a strong and serious man, H. Schliemann, to undertake the excavations that brought to light part of the immense riches of the city of Agamemnon. The amount of gold found in the royal tombs could be compared only with that of the tombs of the Egyptian Pharaohs.

Schliemann was not a scholar in the modern sense of the term. He was a wealthy merchant with extensive classical reading and a command of many languages. His wealth permitted him to satisfy the passion of his life, which was to rediscover the places where the Homeric heroes had lived, fought and died - Troy and Mycenae. As early as 1871 he began excavations in Troy and in 1874, for a short while, in Mycenae. On August 7, 1876, he resumed the excavation in Mycenae with 63 workmen. In the following months of the same year he hit upon the first royal grave, followed by four others containing a total of 15 skeletons of dead Mycenaeans. On November 28, 1876, brimming with enthusiasm, he sent the following cable to the king of Greece, George, announcing his great discovery: "I am very happy to announce to Your Majesty that I have found the monuments which the tradition proclaimed by Pausanias suggests are the graves of Agamemnon, Cassandra, Eurymedon and their associates, all murdered during a meal by Clytemnestra and her lover Aegisthos. These graves are surrounded by a double, parallel circle of slabs, no doubt made in honour of the said high personages. In the tombs, I found an immense treasure of archaeological objects of pure gold. This treasure alone is sufficient to fill a large museum which will be the most splendid in the world and will, in centuries to come, attract myriads of foreigners from every country to Greece..."

Though Schliemann's interpretation of his discoveries was mistaken and caused the mistrust and opposition of many noted scientists, continued research in Mycenae by Schliemann's co-worker Stamatakis and later by Christos Tsountas, along with excavations undertaken in other parts of Greece, have eventually provided a firm basis for the study of Mycenaean civilisation - a civilisation which, as believed from the first and as irrefutably proven later by the decipherment of the Mycenaean script, was a purely Greek one.

Schliemann explored five shaft-graves in the precinct contained within the acropolis of Mycenae, and Stamatakis explored one. These graves numbered with the Roman numerals I-VI, enclosed 19 dead, of whom nine were men, eight were women and two were children. This precinct is referred to as Grave precinct A, to distinguish it from Precinct B.

In 1951, a second grave precinct was discovered outside the acropolis, next to the beehive tomb of "Clytemnestra". Its excavation, which attracted world-wide interest, lasted until 1954. In Precinct B, as the latter was designated to keep it distinct from the earlier one explored by Schliemann, 24 graves including 14 shaft-graves, were found. These graves were numbered with the letters of the Greek alphabet from A to Φ.

The chronology of the Mycenaean period has been determined fairly ac - curately:

1600-1500   early Mycenaean period
1500-1400   middle Mycenaean period
1400-1100   late Mycenaean period

The explosion of the volcano of Thera, an event of grave consequences to the Mycenaean world, is believed to have occurred in the year 1500 B.C., while the expedition of Troy is dated to 1200 B.C.

Collected in the Mycenaean Room of the National Museum are the most important finds from excavations conducted in various centres of Mycenaean Greece. The most striking are the incomparable finds from the royal graves explored by Schliemann and from those discovered much later, in 1951, by I. Papadimitriou. But the rest of the Peloponnese and most of all Attica have also yielded a multitude of important objects, a total of unique value for the study of an age surrounded by legend and poetry.

Owing to the very large number of exhibits in this room, it is obviously impossible to attempt a detailed description of each; only the most significant or the most beautiful will therefore be discussed.

Show-case 1: The ancient legend of the gold of Mycenae was confirmed by the very large number of gold objects found in the Mycenaean graves. Many of these were of funeral use, others were furniture accessories, like the seated gold bull **2947** with gold discs hanging on its horns, which was found in a chambered tomb of the 14th c. B.C. in Mycenae. The bull was a popular theme in Minoan and Mycenaean art, and excellent representations of this animal have been preserved on frescoes, utensils or plastic works, such as the famous cups of Vafion or the silver bullhead-shaped rhyton we will see here. The special significance of the bull in the Mycenaean period is associated with the exceptional physical forces embodied in this animal. This particular appreciation of the bull survived into the classical period, when the bull was regarded as the most choice offering to the gods and its sculptural representations were second only to those of the lion in frequency. **2946:** A gold amulet of the 14th c. B.C. from Mycenae; it is made up of two gold plates and represents a standing bare-breasted woman who holds a decorated object, possibly a box, in her hands; gold grains are used to indicate dress detail, the necklace, and the elaborately arranged hair falling in tresses over the back. **3179:** Gold seal-ring from a chambered tomb of Mycenae, 15th - 14th c. B.C.; a woman in the middle is engaged in a religious dance, a man is shaking a tree on the left, and another woman on the right is lamenting while she crouches on a bench.

11. Cycladic pan-shaped utensil No 6184, from Syros.

12. Steatite pyksis No 5358, from Naxos.

13. Cylindrical vase base depicting fishermen No 5782, from Melos.

14. Five Mycenaean gold seal rings: No 6209, abduction of a woman with ship to the left; No 2971, representation of "holy conversation"; No 241, four men in fight; No 240 two men on chariot hunting deer; No 992, religious scene known as "Minoan pantheon".

15. Miniature sculpture No 2468 of ivory, depicting head of Mycenaean warrior with helmet of boar tusk.

Show-case 20, No 2468: Ivory was a material highly appreciated by the ancients and used in making valuable objects or works of art. Two of the most celebrated works in antiquity were the gold and ivory statues of Zeus in Olympia and of Athena on the Acropolis of Athens, both made by Pheidias. In the Mycenaean period, the material was profusely used, mainly in miniature works of art, such as No **2468,** from a chambered tomb in Mycenae (14th c. B.C.); it represents the head of a warrior wearing a helmet made of wild boar tusk with side pieces joined under the chin. The Mycenaean artist has vividly rendered the features of his model; the head looks alive and that impression is enhanced by the eye, where the pupil was made from a different, coloured material. A colourful description of such a helmet can be found in Homer's Iliad (K 260-265): the helmet described is that of Merionis, a hero from Crete:

And Meriones gave to Odysseus a bow and a quiver and a sword, and about his head he set a helm wrought of hide, and with many a tight-stretched thong was it thick on this side and that, well and cunningly, and within was fixed a lining of felt.

(transl. A.T. Murray).

2489. Famous one-handled silver cup of the 13th century B.C. from a

Mycenaean grave; encircling the cup below the rim is a band showing male heads in left side view (there were 21 heads in all); the technique is that of inlay decoration using niello (a black substance consisting of various oxides).

Show-case 27: Finds from tomb IV of Mycenae. **384:** silver rhyton in the form of a bull-head; a rhyton was a ceremonial vase with a hole in the bottom, through which libations were poured; this particular rhyton is probably the work of a Cretan craftsman, and is dated to the 16th century B.C. ; note the gold horns and the decorative rosette on forehead and muzzle; the use of gold at these points reflects the Mycenaean custom of decorating with gold, or gilding the horns of, actual sacrificial bulls; a similar example is the archaic silver bull of Delphi. **240:** Miniature representations on ring-stones or on the upper surface of Mycenaean rings are important sources of information concerning life and customs in Mycenae. The gold ring No **240** of the first half of the 16th century B.C. shows a hunting scene: two men are in a chariot drawn by two galloping horses and one of them is aiming his arrow at a deer running in front of the chariot; into the tiny elliptical surface of the ring, the craftsman managed to squeeze the chariot and horses, the hunters, the deer, and the scenery, all in the conventional perspective of his time. **253, 254, 259:** Three gold funeral masks; **481:** Silver rhyton of the first half of the 16th century B.C.; this conical rhyton is one of the most celebrated works of Mycenaean gold-smithery; it shows a raised, though not intact, siege scene: depicted on the right is the town surrounded by its walls; crowds of women on the towers wave encouragingly; some trees can be seen on the left; below, the defenders, naked, and armed with slings (standing) or bows (kneeling) are shooting in the opposite direction; some are wearing helmets. The scene probably commemorates some historical event at which the dead man for whom the rhyton was meant, had played a leading part. **351:** Gold cup of the middle of the 16th century B.C. made by forging, a technique that allowed a relatively small quantity of gold to be spread into a thin sheet subsequently shaped into various utensils; the ornamental double rosettes are made by "knocking off", a technique similar to forging; the base and the handle are point-decorated. **412:** Gold vessel with high stem and two handles, of the middle of the 16th century B.C., known as "Nestor's cup" because of the round carved pigeons on the handles answering the Homeric (Iliad: Λ 632-635) description of the cup of Nestor, king of Pylos. **241:** Gold seal-ring of the 16th c. B.C. depicting four fighting men: the two in the middle are contending with swords and one has been forced to his knees; a third man wearing a body-length shield and a helmet and carrying a javelin is striking at the standing fighter; a fourth man, naked and unarmed, is lying on the ground. **394:** War activities are very prominent in the Mycenaean civilisation, witness the frequent war scenes on vases, the daggers and swords found in graves, and of course the Homeric epic Iliad (where a particular period of that civilisation is described). The copper dagger **394** from the Mycenaean grave IV, dating from the 16th c. B.C. not only is a war weapon itself but is ornamented with a war-like scene: one side of the dagger shows a lion hunt in the form of an inlay of silver, gold and black niello: a lion is rushing upon four men who fight it with spears and bows while their bodies are protected with huge figure-of-eight and tower-shaped shields; another man lies on the ground; two other lions are moving off the scene to the right. The other side of the dagger shows a lion attacking antilope.

Show-case 24. 273: Gold forged rhyton in the shape of a lion head, from grave IV of Mycenae, dating from the first half of the 16th c. B.C. **294:** Copper dagger with a finely worked gold handle and a cylindrical upper part; the technique used is the "cloisonnée", which consists in filling the spaces of the gold latticework covering

16. Seated gold bull No 2947, with gold discs hanging from horns.

17. Silver bull head No 384 with gold horns and gold rosette, used as rhyton.

18. Bronze Mycenaean daggers with representations: No 8339, nautilus amidst rocks; 394, lion hunt; 744, engraved spiral.

the handle with chips of lapis lazuli and rock crystal. The latticework terminates in two open-mouthed dragon-heads facing each other. 16th century B.C.

Show-case 4. 808: Hexagonal wooden box *(pyxis)* from grave V of Mycenae, dating from the 16th century B.C.; each side of the hexagon is coated on the outside with two moulded gold sheets decorated with scenes of lions chasing deer or with spirals. **623:** Gold death mask.

Funeral stele, 1428. Funeral steles were found over the two circular precincts of Mycenae; of the many discovered by Schliemann in grave circle A, several bore relief decorations, while others were totally unadorned. Identical steles were also found in grave circle B. Opinions vary as to the significance of the unadorned steles but there is serious evidence in support of the theory that they were erected over the graves of women. The steles with bas-relief decoration generally show scenes with armed men and chariots, i.e. hunting or war scenes. This stele No **1428** of the 16th cent. B.C. has on its upper part three rows of continuous and intertwined spirals, while the lower part shows a chariot race; in front of the horse, a male figure is picking up some object, possibly a shield; these scenes on the Mycenaean steles are presumed to represent chariot races held in honour of the dead buried in the graves concerned.

Show-case 3. 624: Five male gold masks were found, as reported by Schliemann, on as many skulls in graves IV and V of Mycenae; the faces of two small children found in grave III were also covered with masks, though these were less elaborate and were made of a thinner sheet of gold. The heads of dead women were not covered with masks but were adorned with diadems and bands.

The moulded gold mask No **624** from grave V of Mycenae, dating from the middle of the 16th c. B.C., with engraved facial details (eyebrows, moustache and beard) is the most valued and perhaps the best known find from the graves of circle A. In his enthusiasm over the discovery of the royal graves of Mycenae, Schliemann maintained that it was the death mask of Agamemnon, the leader of the Greeks in the expedition of Troy and is still often, though wrongly, referred to as the mask of Agamemnon. The pronounced and very personal features of the mask, suggesting a dignified and mild man, would indeed be well suited to the war chief of the Achaeans and king of Mycenae, Agamemnon; but there is positive historical evidence that his reign and the Trojan war occurred much later than the 16th century to which the mask is dated. So Schliemann's theory, attractive as it may be, is unfounded.

Show-case 23. 1: Gold diadem from grave III of Mycenae, belonging to a dead princess. It is decorated with moulded rosettes and is fitted with gold pieces forming nine flower calyces. **3, 5:** Diamond-shaped gold diadem decorated with seven moulded circular gold discs. Seven wedge-like similarly decorated pieces were fitted to its upper part. The purpose of this diadem was purely funeral; second half of the 16th c. B.C. **70, 91:** Small gold scales (replica) from grave III of Mycenae, made of gold sheet pieces; it is probably connected with the "psychostasia" = the weighing of souls, an example of which we find in the Iliad (X 209 ff) where Zeus weighs on gold scales the destinies of Achilles and Hector to decide which is to die first. **33:** Gold seal-ring from grave III of Mycenae; a man armed with a sword strikes at a charging lion; 16th c. B.C.

Show-case 22. 552: Ostrich egg converted into a rhyton by the addition of a faïence mouth and neck decorated with moulded spirals, from grave IV of Mycenae. Similar rhytons found, apart from Mycenae, in Midea and recently in Thera, bear witness to the existence of trade relations between Egypt and Mycenae, though according to Prof. Marinatos, these eggs came from Syria. It is not clear whether they reached Greece in rhyton form or the faïence additions were made here; middle of 16th c. B.C. **389:** From grave IV of Mycenae: Excellent alabaster vase with three added handles, also of alabaster, S-shaped with a closed upper curve; with its short widening stem, the broad body, the narrowing neck ending in a wavy rim, all of these are somewhat reminiscent of the classical crater in terms of shape. Excellent work of the middle of the 16th century B.C., an example of the metal vessel technique applied to stone.

Show-case 28. 146: Gold sheets from grave III of Mycenae, used to cover the entire body of a dead baby (found in grave III were the skeletons of three women and two twin infants). Note that several body details are indicated including the eyes, the mouth, the ears, and the fingers and toes. Second half of the 16th century B.C.

Show-case 5. 8638: Perhaps the most famous find from the excavation of the graves of circle B in Mycenae explored by I. Papadimitriou, is the vase No **8638,**

made from rock crystal and found in grave O, a woman's grave as indicated by other objects contained in it. The vase is in the shape of a duck, whose body forms the actual vase, while the head and neck are turned towards the interior forming the handle. It has been noted (G. Mylonas) that; "the skill with which the shape of the bird was adapted to the form of the vase, the fine workmanship, the clear-cut contours and the thinness of the walls, make of this vase an outstanding work of art". The bronze brooches **8635-7** with crystal heads were found in the same grave. This grave contained indeed so many crystal objects that it is sometimes referred to as the "crystal grave".

Show-case 21. 2665: Fragment of a miniature fresco from the so-called "Tsountas House" on the acropolis of Mycenae, dating from the 14th century. Represented are three demons with ass heads carrying a horizontal piece of timber or rope resting on their shoulders. Demons are a frequent motif in Mycenaean art.

Base 4575. Female head (0,168 m high) of brightly coloured plaster, one of the very few examples of round sculptures of that size from the Mycenaean period. The pale complexion is a conventional indication that the head is that of a woman; it may be that of a sphinx, a very popular theme in the late Mycenaean period. Facial features, such as the eyebrows, eyes, lips and hair are painted in bright colours; another ornament, possibly reflecting a real tattoo, consists of punctuated rosettes on the cheeks, chin and forehead. Found in a Mycenaean house by Tsountas and dated to the 13th century B.C.

3256. Funeral stele of sandstone, made in the 16th century B.C. and decorated with engraved ornaments. Centuries after its first use, it was employed again for the same purpose in the 13th c. B.C. Its decorated surface was covered with white plaster and painted with rows of pictures, two of which have been well preserved and show animals and warriors.

Show-case 6. 8708: Seal-stone of amethyst from grave Γ of Mycenae, with carved, portrait-like head of a man with well-pronounced facial features. He wears a beard and long hair, the eye is visible in its entirety and the lines of the face are typical of what has come to be known as the "Greek type". According to G. Mylonas, this portrait may be representative of the Mycenaean ruler in general. This lense-shaped seal-stone was carved by a Cretan craftsman and is dated to the early 16th century B.C.

The number of Mycenaean seals and the variety of themes in their illustrations are so great, that a special branch of Mycenaean archaeology is dedicated to their study. The Mycenaean seals differ from those of Crete in both styles and subjects: wild beasts, lions, bulls, imaginary creatures, demons with heads of lions, griffins, sphinxes, religious, hunting, and war scenes are the most frequent in the Mycenaean type of seal.

19. Gold death-masks from Mycenaean tombs 253, 259; *No* 624 *on the right is the so-called "mask of Agamemnon".*

In terms of craftsmanship, the skill of the Mycenaean artists commands respect and admiration: to represent entire scenes on such tiny surfaces is no mean achievement. The art of seal-carving came to Mycenaean Greece at an already advanced stage of development from Crete, but the Mycenaeans adapted its styles and themes to suit their own ideas.

Show-case 30. 992: Gold seal-ring of the 15th c. B.C. from the so-called "treasury" of the acropolis of Mycenae, also known as the "Minoan Pantheon" owing to the incalculable value of its representation as a source of information about the Cretan-Mycenaean religion and worship since it shows many elements of the latter: on the left, sitting under a tree which symbolises a sacred grove, a goddess is shown with little serving maids in front and behind her; she holds some poppies that she has just been offered by a woman still standing before her with outstretched hand; another woman standing behind the first one is, in her turn, going to offer lilies to the goddess; above and between the two women, an armed figure is descending from heaven; the sacred symbol of the double axe is shown in the middle of the picture and high above are the moon and the sun on a wavy line that represents the sky. **957:** Gold cylix with fairly tall cylindrical stem, conical body, and two handles ending in dog-heads that bite the rim of the vase; it is made of forged sheets joined with nails. **7711:** Among Mycenaean sculptures, the fame of this striking round carved ivory group of two embracing women with a young child between them, is second only to the relief of the Gate of Lions. The Cretan-Mycenaean type of the dress and jewellery is of great interest. The religious significance of this sculpture is undoubted, it is known in fact as the "sacred trinity" and, according to prevalent opinion, it represents Demeter, Persephone, and Iacchus i.e. the god who led the procession of initiates at the Eleusinian Mysteries. Early 13th century B.C.

On base, 1426. The best known piece of pottery of the Mycenaean period is the so-called "vase of warriors", a crater with double handles ending in ox heads *(boucrana)*, which was found at the excavation of a Mycenaean house. Represented on the main side of the vase are six warriors with helmets, breastplates and jambs, wearing short tasseled chitons. They are carrying shields and spears and their gait suggests that they are leaving for some expedition, as also indicated by the sacks slung on the spears; a woman waves goodbye on the left. The other side shows five similar warriors. 13th c.B.C.

Show-case 8. 8343: Mirrors, a necessary article of toiletry for women, are fairly frequent in the Mycenaean period. Their form does not differ essentially from that of the masterpieces of the classical age: a bronze disc with a simple or elaborate handle. For many years, the value of the mirror is determined by the quality of workmanship in the handle, as in the case of No **8343**, a mirror of the second half of the 15th century B.C. found in a beehive tomb at Pylos. This ivory handle is decorated with moulded rosettes and was fastened to the bronze disc with nails. **8357:** Another necessary adjunct to female beauty, this comb has a feather-shaped handle and comes from the same beehive tomb as the mirror (first half of the 15th c. B.C.); it is made of ivory engraved with ornamental designs: in a scenery of water plants, cat-like animals are chasing duck.

Show-case 10. 8446: Copper dagger from Prosymna (15th c. B.C.) with an inlay of gold, silver and black niello representing a dolphin on each side.

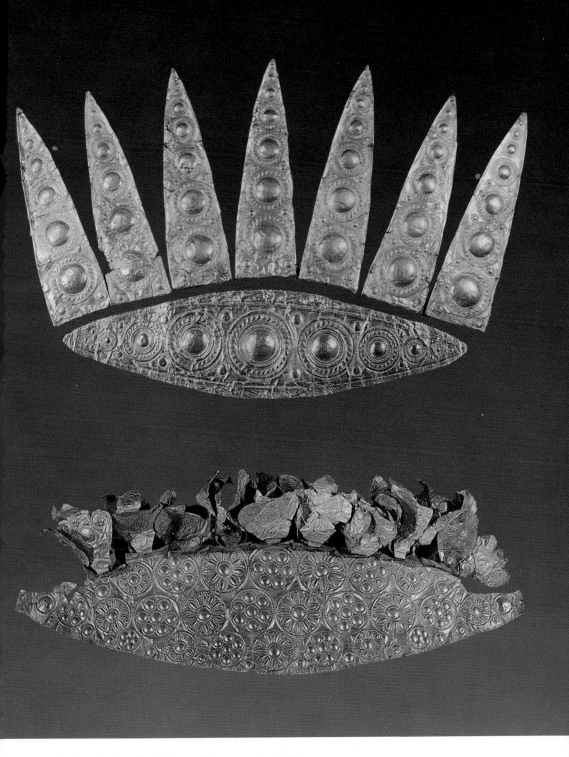

20. *Gold diadem No 3,5 from Mycenaean tomb III.*

21. *Gold diadem No 1 from the same tomb.*

22. Gold seal-ring No 6208 with ritual scene.

23. Gold seal No 33 with likeness of man fighting a lion.

24. Gold seal-ring No 2970 showing two griffins.

25. Gold head of a silver hairpin No 75.

26. Duck-shaped rock crystal vase No 8638.

29

27. *Small ivory relief No 5897 showing woman seated on a rock.*

28. *Ivory group No 7711: two women and an infant.*

29. *Head, probably of sphinx, No 4575, of coloured paste.*

30. *Four bronze Mycenaean swords with precious handles No 7325, 7316, 6444 and 7326.*

Show-case 11. 6416: Copper dagger from Prosymna with an inlay of gold, silver and black niello representing pigeons. **6878:** Pig-shaped clay vase from Prosymna, decorated with reddish-brown lines. 13th century B.C.

Show-case 19. 8556: Rare basket-shaped clay vase from Varkiza, Attica, decorated with fish in a seascape, with upright double handles, of the 15th century B.C. The subject and the shape of the vase suggest Cretan origin. **8557:** This painted clay boot was found by I. Papadimitriou in Alyki Glyfada, Attica, in 1955 in a chambered tomb; it is hollow inside, while the exterior surface is covered with ornamental painting; the tip is nozzle-shaped. Wings are painted on the part covering the ankles, and a brown band on the lower part of the calf indicates the strap used to tie the shoe to the leg. According to I. Papadimitriou, this boot was a ritual-symbolic object, possibly placed in a grave as useful equipment for the deceased's journey to the netherworld. Winged sandals were worn by Hermes in Homeric descriptions, and the same is said of Perseus in Hesiod. 14th century B.C.

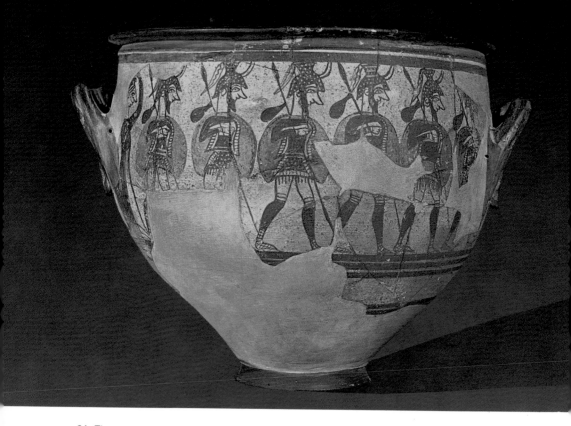

31. *The so-called "vase of warriors" No 1426.* 32. *Crater fragments No 1511 showing chariot and warriors.*

Show-case 32. 1758: One of the few Mycenaean beehive tombs (the tombs of royalty) that have been found intact, was explored by Tsountas in Vafion of Laconia, south of Sparta. Apart from the two famous gold cups with fitted handles we will see in a moment, this grave yielded a wealth of all kinds of burial objects incl. bronze utensils, axes, a bronze sword, a dagger inlaid with gold, knives, beads from an amethyst necklace, silver cups - one in each of the dead man's hands - and many gold and other ornamental objects and weaponry. Gold cup No **1758** is decorated with a highly artistic, naturalistic and skilfully executed scene: capture of wild bulls; it is a compelling and suggestive scene in a conventional land-scape of shrub, trees and rocks. In the middle of the representation, a bull is caught in a trap net, whose ends are tied to two trees; a second bull, to the right, appears to have managed to escape and is fleeing for his life, as suggested by his tense legs; a third bull is galloping off to the left, while a man, an acrobat-tamer, holds precariously onto the beast's horns; a second man is falling backwards, shaken off by the terrible strength of the scared animal. According to Tsountas, the two cups "display all the essential features of Cretan art: the freedom and impetus of movement, the frequently hazardous stance, the slender, flexible and sinewy bodies of the men and, finally, the loving observation and representation of nature in general, and of animal life in particular". **1759:** The scene shown on the second gold cup from Vafion is a peaceful one: a man (on the left) has tied a length of rope to the leg of a bull and is leading him away, while another bull and a cow are engaged in mating in the middle of the picture; a third bull, on the right, appears to have just arrived on the scene. As suggested by the similarity of size and subject, the two cups are the work of the same artist and belong together - they are two of a pair, as observed by Tsountas. They are dated to the 15th century B.C.

Show-case 9: Clay tablets from Pylos. The discovery that the linear designs on the clay tablets found at the excavation of the Mycenaean palace of Pylos represented texts written in the Greek language, was one of the greatest philological and historical discoveries of the postwar period. All of a sudden, there were Greek texts older than Homer. The decipherment of these tablets is due to two Englishmen: the architect M. Ventris and the philologist J. Chadwick. This very ancient script, known as Linear B, uses both the syllabic system and ideograms; mentioned in the tablets are various occupations, names of gods, utensils, fruits.

5883. Restored fragments of a fresco from the later palace of Tiryns: there is a woman who probably carried a box and, together with other women, formed part of a procession moving to the right, possibly to meet with another group moving to the left. The blue background sets off the bright-coloured figures: face and breasts are white; the eyes and the elaborately done hair are black; dress and head ribbons are red. 13th century B.C.

5878-82: Fragments of fresco, restored for the most part, from the later palace of Tiryns: set against a blue background is a multicoloured vivid hunting scene. A wild boar hit on the head with the spear of a hunter, of whose body only a brown hand has been preserved, is trying to escape the dogs surrounding him. The two women on the chariot were perhaps watching the scene. 13th c. B.C.

Show-case 33, 8743: Magnificent gold cup of the 15th century from a chambered tomb in Midea: low base, spherical body decorated with floral motif (ivy leaves) repeated around the rim which is not circular but wavy.

33. *The famous gold cups of Vafio Nos* 1578 *and* 1579.

34. *Gold Mycenaean cups No* 440, 73, 442 *and* 630.

34

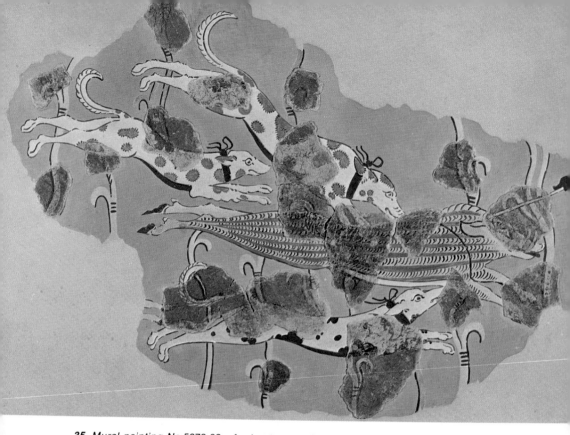

35. *Mural painting No 5878-82 of a hunt scene (partially restored) from Tiryns.*

36. *Mural painting from Mycenae in excellent state of preservation portraying a woman - possibly a goddess.*

Show-case 14: This fragment of fresco depicting a woman, was found at the latest excavation of Mycenae (1970). G. Mylonas, who discovered it, has called it "The Mycenaean Lady" and has pointed out its "archaic grace and dignity". The fragment itself is well-preserved but represents only such a small part of the whole that no hypothesis can be advanced as to the subject of the representation. The distinguished and authoritative appearance of the woman have given rise to various speculations, the most prevalent view being that she is a goddess.

On a blue background, the figure is painted in bright colours - white for the bare parts of the body, and brown, purple and white for the rich dress; jewels adorn the wrists and the neck, while the elaborate hairdo is kept in place with ribbons. This is undoubtedly the best preserved fresco of Mycenaean Greece found so far. A remarkable feature, occurring also in the art of later periods, is that the body is shown in front view while the head is seen from the side. 13th century B.C.

Show-case 15. 6208: Gold seal-ring from the so-called "treasury of Tiryns", dating from the 15th century B.C.: four demons with lion features are carrying libation vases and proceed toward an enthroned woman (goddess) who is holding up a broad-mouthed vase in her raised right hand; in front of her on a high stem is an incense-burner. The woman's feet rest on a footstool and behind her there is a bird. Drops of rain, the sun and the moon are shown high up in the sky, but they are separated by branches; small trees and ears of corn are shooting up between the demons. There is an ornamental frieze below the main representation. This ring is one of the most highly appreciated relics of Mycenaean art and is of particular importance for the study of religion; it is accepted by the majority of experts that the scene represents some kind of ritual connected with vegetation, fertility and produce of the earth - a problem of paramount importance for primitive man who was wholly dependent on nature for his survival. **1511.** Joined fragments of a clay vase of the 13th century from Tiryns. Pictured on it are a war chariot, two warriors with spears and shields in front of it, and a dog under the horses; two different techniques are involved in the painting: the bodies are filled with colour and decorated with wavy lines, whereas the heads of the men and the animals consist only of the contours with the eyes marked within them. Though approximately contemporary with the "vase of warriors" No **1426,** the painting in this case is of inferior quality and cannot compete with the other in boldness of outline, movement of the warriors, and story-telling style.

Show-case 16. 6444: Found in a tomb in Scopelos, the ancient Peparethos and the largest island of the North Sporades group, this bronze sword has a gold handle made of gold sheets attached to an interior core. The decoration of the handle, consisting mainly of spirals, is raised and covers the entire surface. The sword accompanied some princely person of Mycenaean Scopelos to his grave. From legends, we know that the island had relations with Crete: it is said to have been first settled by Cretans from Knossos led by Staphylos, who was the son of Ariadne and Dionyssos or Theseus, one of the Argonauts. 15th century B.C.

36

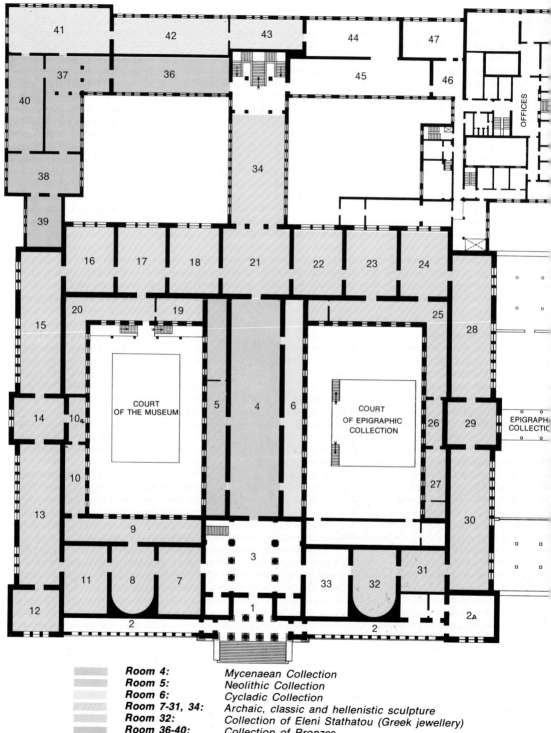

	Room 4:	Mycenaean Collection
	Room 5:	Neolithic Collection
	Room 6:	Cycladic Collection
	Room 7-31, 34:	Archaic, classic and hellenistic sculpture
	Room 32:	Collection of Eleni Stathatou (Greek jewellery)
	Room 36-40:	Collection of Bronzes
	Room 41-43:	Collection of Sculptures of the Roman period

(redrawing by John Travlos)

THE COLLECTION OF SCULPTURES

The collection of sculptures is the most important part of the National Museum, representing a large part of the monumental art of the Greeks from its remotest archaic period down to its last revival in the early Christian era. The main body of the exhibition is made up of sculptural works found in Attica. Additional knowledge of Attic sculptural art can be gained from exhibits in the museum of the Acropolis and from the considerable collections kept in local museums in the area of Attica.

As far as archaic sculpture is concerned, the exhibits in the National Museum are again representative; further insights can be obtained from the sculptural complexes in the two great centres of Hellenism: Olympia and Delphi. Important individual works can also be seen in other museums. Examples are the sculptures of the pediment from the temple of Apollo Daphnephoros at Eretria kept in the museum of Chalkis, and sculptures from islands, such as Samos, Naxos, Corfu.

Sculpture is the most prominent expression of the classical art par excellence, namely the art of the ancient Greeks. Painting was probably no less developed but its products, executed in perishable materials, have been lost and only echoes of that art have been preserved on vessels, Attic vessels of the archaic and the classic periods, in particular. Sculpture had a place in every aspect of the life of the Greeks, especially of the Athenians: sculptures adorned their temples, and the ceremonial likenesses of their gods were statues; statuary or sculpture in relief was used to decorate tombs and to honour the dead. It is in fact the large place occupied by this art in the lives of the people that explains the large number of works preserved, as well as the resplendent course of the art and the birth of so many great artists — true giants of the human spirit.

From the Middle Ages onwards, the West began to take an interest in all things Greek — spiritual as well as economic and political. Travellers started touring the Greek territorries then under Turkish rule; in their books, they tell of their interest in Ancient Greece and of how they tried to find its vestiges with the aid of ancient geographers, travellers and historians. All the West knew of ancient art at the time were the works — statues, houses — that existed in Italy; it had never seen an original classical Greek sculpture. The discovery, on January 14, 1506, before Michelangelo's amazed eyes, of the Laocoon group in Rome, was a revelation for the West, and this first acquaintance with a great Greek work was to have a profound influence on European art. However, classical Attic art was only to become known to the West through the marbles removed from the Parthenon by lord Elgin, when Athens was still under Turkish rule. Elgin's marbles first became accessible to artists and art-lovers in April 1810. The impression they made is best expressed in the words of the English painter B.R. Haydon: "I never shall forget the horses' heads the feet in the metops! I felt as if a divine truth had blazed inwardly upon my mind, and I knew that they would at last rouse the art of Europe from its slumber in the darkness... I drew at the marbles ten, fourteen, fifteen hours at a time, staying often till twelve at night, holding a candle and my board in one hand, and drawing with the other".

Just like the Parthenon marbles, the sculptures in the National Museum are important because they are genuine and original works, direct testimonies of the life and art of the ancient Greeks. They provide artistic and historical information that is essential to the understanding of this people. Each work has a definite place in

ancient history and each is the product of a determined historical moment and necessity. The study and knowledge of these sculptural works makes the remote world of the ancients a near and familiar one: its better understanding helps us to better understand our own times and ourselves.

Room 7, of Nikandra

Quite a number of larger works of the earliest monumental art of the Greeks, the so-called "daedalic" art, have been preserved, such as Nikandra's offering, the kore of Auxerre, the sitting statue from Agiorgitica in Arcadia, but, mainly, we have a profusion of small clay or bronze figurines.

Naturally, Greek art was not created overnight and the works we will see in the first room of sculpture were not the first made by Greek craftsmen. Before them, there was the earlier period known as "geometric", when statues erected in temples were referred to as "xoana": one "xoanon" representing Herakles was seen by the traveller Pausanias (2nd c. A.D.) near the theatre of Corinth. Says Pausanias: *"This is said to be a work of Daedalos. All works made by Daedalos are somewhat strange in appearance, but there is something divine in them"*. This divine character of the earlier works can still be detected in the small ivory, bronze or clay figurines and in some of the larger marble works which preserve many elements of the style and features of the venerable statues that Greek tradition attributes to that legendary Athenian sculptor, Daedalos. *"Daedalos,"* says one ancient writer, *"was an excellent architect and the first inventor of statues"*. But the greatest achievement of Daedalos — and the statement holds true of all sculptors of that very

39

37. *Porous metope No 2869 from the temple of Athena (7th c. B.C.) in Mycenae.*

38. *Ivory statuette of nude woman No 776 from Dipylon.*

39. *The female statue No 1 from Delos dedicated by Nikandra to Artemis.*

early period — was that his skill was such as to make the ancients believe that statues could move and talk.

804. The best abilities of the artists of the geometric period — that was the time when the Homeric poems took concrete form — are not to be sought in the small metal objects or small-size ceramics, but in the huge vessels of Dipylon: in terms of size, these vessels seem to reflect the artist's audacity, and his pride in being able to bring off his bold project. This famous funeral amphora from Dipylon near Athens, is the perfect expression of this type of Greek plastic art.

The dense decoration in belts allows the eye no rest. The dark belts around the mouth are succeeded by others with meanders and grazing animals. Spread out between the handles is the main theme: the deceased on his death-bed in the middle, with men and women mourners around and underneath. The decoration continues with bands and meanders. It is evident that the death scene, occupying such a small part of the vessel's surface, was meant only to indicate its use. The vessel itself would impress the viewer by its sheer size and by its harmonious and dynamic form. No less admirable than the ability of the potter is the skill of the painter, who is known by the conventional name "painter of Dipylon". Middle 8th c. B.C.

2869. On the site of the palace of Mycenae, a Doric temple had been built in the later half of the 7th century (there is an inscription suggesting that Athena was worshipped in Mycenae as early as the archaic period), and from this temple we have a number of porous stone sculptures — metopes according to the prevailing opinion. No **2869** represents an advanced stage of Daedalic art; it is a veiled goddess with covered head. The facial features are chiselled and there is a hint of the archaic smile. Also from this building, metope **2870** is a fragmentary representation of a naked man with wild beasts, and metope **4471,** showing remains of the figure of a warrior. About 630 B.C.

776. Five ivory statuettes have been preserved from the tomb of Dipylon, representing nude women. No **776** has a "polos" on the head, decorated with a meander design in relief; the arms stick to the body, the waist is slender, the legs are close together. Other finds from the same tomb (geometric vessels) determine the date of the statuette (abt. 750 B.C.).

1. The female statue dedicated by the woman Nikandra from Naxos to the great sanctuary of Apollo in Delos, dates from the middle of the 7th century B.C. It is the work of a Naxian sculptor and represents Artemis. The xoanon-like shape, the arms sticking to the body and the legs kept close together, express the Daedalic spirit of the earliest archaic Ionic plastic art. Engraved on the left side is the famous inscription: *I was dedicated to the goddess who enjoys throwing her arrows afar by Nikandra, daughter of Deinodikos of Naxos, the best among women, sister of Deinomenes and now wife of Fraxos.* The laudatory tone of the inscription suggests that Nikandra's family belonged to the aristocracy of Naxos, but that is also evident from the size and the value of the offering. Interestingly, the inscription has the statue itself speaking on behalf of the donor — a custom of the Greeks of the archaic period, which has produced a number of interesting texts like the one just quoted.

56. Memorial stele from Tanagra in Boeotia. Two young men, Kitylos and Dermys, are shown in an embrace, each with an arm around the other's neck, and one foot forward. On the front of the pedestal on which they stand is the inscription: Ἀμφάλκες μὲ στασι ἐπὶ Κιτύλοι ἐδ' ἐπὶ Δέρμυι. (Amphakles dedicated me, in memory of Dermys and Kitylos). On the far surface of the stele, the names are again engraved to show which figure is which man: Dermys on the left, Kitylos on the right. Middle 6th century B.C.

57. Porous stone statue of a sitting woman, found in the village Agiorgitica near Tegea in the district of Arcadia. It wears a short-sleeved chiton and a thick himation with a border of finely worked sash. The head is turned to the left, a movement that lends vividness to the work; but the face is badly damaged. A superb post-Daedalic work with shoulders and arms of exquisite plasticity, it must have inspired respect and awe by its still impressive dignity. It may represent a dead woman (memorial statue) or, more likely, the goddess Demeter. It is indeed believed, based on a passage in Pausanias, that a sanctuary of that goddess existed at the site where the statue was found, near the ancient road leading from Tegea to Argos. About 630 B.C.

In the following rooms, we will see a series of statues of standing naked young men, the left foot a little forward as if they were going to take a step. Statues of this type are known as "kouroi" (a "kouros" in ancient Greek is a boy, youth or child). The name "kouros" was never used by the ancients themselves in connection with these statues. It was first introduced by a Greek archaeologist, Vassilios Leonardos in 1895 to designate the kouros No 1904 from Keratea (Room 13).

"The type of kouros, a standing youth, also referred to as archaic Apollo, is encountered in ancient Greek sculpture like a leitmotiv in music. It appears with the beginning of Greek sculpture and develops throughout the period of Greek archaic art. We find it in Asia Minor, in the islands, in continental Greece, in North Africa and in the West — everywhere in the Greek world. The kouros occurs wherever Greek sculptors were at work, wherever the Greek civilization flourished" (G. Richter).

It would appear that this type of statue was taken over by the Greeks from Ancient Egypt, where great sculpture had blossomed long before. However the Greek artists, unlike their Egyptian counterparts who remained captive even to the shape of the stone they used for their statues, were soon able to gain mastery over their materials and, later, to take advantage of the greater freedom afforded by bronze.

Thus the type of the standing male statue remained static with the Egyptians, but it became a subject of continuing interest with the Greeks. "The main concern of archaic plastic art was how to represent in a worthy manner that highest Greek ideal, the young male body — the *andropais*" (K. Romeos). And, as K. Romeos correctly points out, there can be no more fitting description of a kouros than the words of Aeschylus concerning the youth Parthenopaeos in "Seven Against Thebes":

τὸδ αὐδᾷ μητρὸς ἐξ ὀρεσκόου
βλάστημα καλλίπρῳρον, ἀνδρόπαις ἀνήρ.
στείχει δ' ἴουλος ἄρτι διὰ παρηΐδων
ὥρας φυούσης, ταρφὺς ἀντέλλουσα θρίξ.

"So spake he, the well-built sprout of a mountain-bred mother, the gallant man-child..."

Room 8, of the Kouros of Sounion

3372. Ushering the impressive series of Attic kouroi in the National Museum is the larger-than-life "Dipylon Head" (about 610 B.C.) from a statue that stood on the tomb of some young Athenian nobleman. The large size is a reflection of the idea of greatness that prevailed among the aristocratic families of Attica in the time of Draco.

Separated from the body, which has not been preserved, the head seems surrounded by mystery despite the wide-open eyes. The fact that it was originally thought to be the head of a Sphinx is suggestive. The hair is geometric in shape, executed in the form of small chips, though these are not absolutely symmetrical. "Although self-contained, the large, salient astragals rhythmically combine with one another into a polyphonal harmonious melody" (K. Romeos). It is held with a band tied in a knot at the back of the head. A similar knot tied in the oposite direction will be seen in the kouros of Sounion.

2720. At the SE extremity of Attica, on Cape Sounion, there are the ruins of a sanctuary of Poseidon. The white columns of the god's temple on the uppermost part of the Cape were a familiar landmark to travellers sailing by across the frequently rough sea. Excavations carried out by Greeks in 1906 brought to light east of the temple a cache containing kouros 2720, the trunk of kouros 3645, several fragments of arms and legs of statues and some statue bases, buried there by the ancients after the destruction of the archaic temple by the Persians in 480 B.C.

Kouros **2720** is of supernatural and indeed of gigantic size (3,05m tall) and is intact. By some fortunate accident, even the plinth and the base have been preserved. The shape of the body is angular and robust. The stylized hair spreads out in locks made up of apparently symmetrical astragals and is held by a band tied in a knot at the back (Herculian knot). The chest is broad and the waist is narrow; many anatomical details are indicated by grooves and nervures below the chest and, to a greater extent, on the back and on the dorsal aspects of the hands. Note the stylized form of the ear, a markedly archaic feature also present in the Dipylon head. This kouros, an impressive offering to Poseidon, represents no longer the "dawn of Greek plastic art but its brilliant morning" (G. Richter). Though archaic, it strongly and fully embodies what was one of the main aspirations of Greek artists — perfection in the rendering of the naked male body in marble.

353. The so-called "amphora of Piraeus" comes from a grave (about 630 B.C.); it is a black-figured vessel showing a cock and two chariots, each drawn by two horses (*diphroi*). The style of the animals with their inflexible legs ("wooden legs" as they have been described) reflects the stage in painting which corresponds to that of sculpture in the period between Kylon and Draco.

3645. The second kouros from the sanctuary of Poseidon in Sounion is smaller and less well-preserved but displays the same features as No 2720: a broad chest, a narrow waist, grooves to indicate anatomical details. The strands of hair end in spirals. Believed to be the work of the same sculptor as kouros 2720. About 600 B.C.

4/3443. "Perirrhanteria" were ceremonial utensils in Greek sanctuaries; they were used to sprinkle water for purification or sacrificial purposes; they were also objects that could be offered to the gods, especially when they were made of precious materials, like the two "perirrhanteria", one of gold and one of silver, dedicated by Croesus to Apollo in Delphi as reported by Herodotus. In most cases, they were relatively flat bowls supported by a small column. In earlier periods, these columns were sometimes shaped like human forms. The two xoanon-like female statuettes from the sanctuary of Apollo on Mt. Ptoon were, together with a third one which has not been preserved, such sprinkler-bowl supports. The figure wears a veil girdled about the hips (*bathyzonous*), the arms go straight down close to the body with the fingers spread apart. Late 7th century B.C.

2. Statue trunk with floor-length high-girdled chiton and himation, xoanon-like and nearly rectangular, made of limestone. It was found in Apollo's sanctuary on Mt. Ptoon. Engraved in the lower part in the "ox-turn" style (reading from left to right, then, in the next line, from right to left) is a votive inscription — one of the earliest Greek inscriptions — including mention of the sculptor: *[...] qov αναθεκε τοι Απολ/ονι τοι Πτοει/ [...]οτοσ εποιFεσε.* (..phon dedicated to Apollo of Ptoon; ...otos made it).

When the statue was found in 1885, traces of red colour were still visible on the left foot. Late 7th century B.C.

On Mt. Ptoon of Boeotia, east of Copais and below the Pelagia monastery, there are the ruins of an oracle of Apollo, which was of considerable importance in antiquity, especially for Boeotia. Musical and athletic contests were held there in honour of the god. Excavations conducted by the French School of Archaeology brought to light not only vestiges of buildings but also several valuable sculptures; the most important of these are a series of kouroi or heads of kouroi dedicated to Apollo; a number of these sculptures will be seen in the National Museum, others, of secondary importance, are kept in the museum of Thebes.

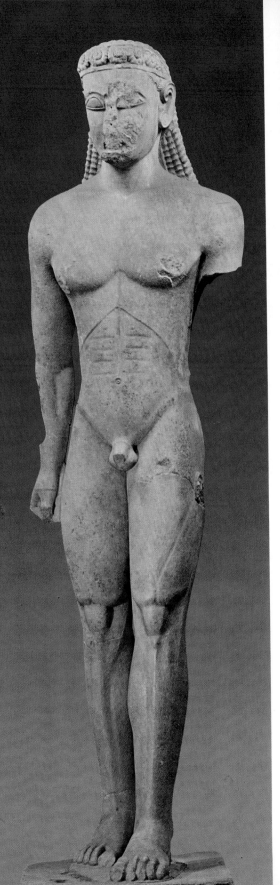

40. *The giant kouros No 2720 from the sanctuary of Poseidon in Sounion.*

41. *The excellent "head of Dipylon" No 3372 from a kouros of the late 7th c. B.C.*

40

15. This porous stone head from Ptoon was discovered in 1885. It is made of local white limestone resembling marble. The hair is stylized and tied with a band but does not show the sculptor's meticulous care noted in the Dipylon head and in the kouroi of Sounion. The ear is flat, with no attempt to depict detail. The facial features are strongly pronounced, lending the face what might be described as a personal expression.

As far back as 1890, the then Curator General of Antiquities Panayotis Kavvadias had expressed the opinion that this head was made using the "xoanon" technique. "Possibly", he wrote, "it is a copy of a previous wooden work; or, more likely, the craftsman was accustomed to working with wood and, being inexperienced in the more demanding task of working with hard stone, he used his familiar wood-carving technique". This view, which was not heeded at the time, is now gaining acceptance among the younger generation of investigators. About 580 B.C.

Room 9, of Phrasikleia

4889. This female statue discovered at Merenda in the Mesogeia area of Attica in 1972, is an important though not surprising find, considering that it comes from Attica. It dates from about 540 B.C. and is the work of Aristion, a well-known sculptor of the archaic period and a native of Paros. This "kore", erected on the tomb of a

42. *Sphinx No 28 from Spata. Attica; it served as crown of a funerary stele.*

43. *Statue of Winged Nike No 21 from Delos - a pediment of some building in the sanctuary of Apollo.*

woman named Phrasikleia, wears the Ionic chiton which she holds with her left hand, the other arm bent on the chest and holding a flower in its finger-tips. The head is adorned with earrings and wears a crown made of calyces and lotus flowers; there is a necklace around the neck. The dress is decorated with meanders, rosettes and swastikas — a decorative element found also in black-figured pottery. Engraved on the (long-known) base of the statue is the elegiac epigram to the young woman, which is famous for its possible interpretations: *Σεμα Φρασικλείας. Κόρε κεκλέσομαι αἰεὶ / ἀντὶ γάμο παρὰ θεὸν τοῦτο λαχόσ' ὄνομα. / ['Αρεσ]τίον: Πάριος ἐπ]ο[ίε]σε.*

Found together with the statue of the girl was kouros No **4890** kept in the adjacent room. The fact that the two statues were found together has suggested the hypothesis that they were made by the same sculptor and represented a brother and sister—obviously a hard to prove assumption.

A type of statue often encountered in archaic Greek sculpture alongside that of the kouros, is the "kore", or statue of a young woman. Such statues would be erected on tombs as sepulchral monuments or in sanctuaries as offerings to gods and goddesses. An exquisite series of "kore" statues, unique in the variety of artistic tendencies they represent and in the preservation of their ancient colours so alien to modern aesthetics (the kore from Phrasikleia's grave also preserves some traces of colour) were found on the Acropolis and are on display in that museum.

59

21. The small statue found in Delos in 1877 represents Nike who, according to Hesiod, was the slim-ankled daughter of the Titan Pallas and of Styx. The sculptor has depicted her in flight, with legs bent and suspended in the air. There were wings on her shoulders and feet. She is wearing a chiton, blown between her legs by the wind; the now plain upper part would probably have been adorned with painted on jewellery. The statue rested on its plinth supported by the hem of the dress, a stance which must have seemed an original one and indeed a bold artistic innovation in its time. Otherwise, however, the statue is conventionally archaic, with the upper part of the body being looked at from the front, the lower part from the side. The statue served as an acroterium in some building or temple in Delos. At one time there was a suggestion, now rejected, that the statue belonged to the base No 21a, which comes also from Delos and is inscribed with a three-verse epigram in hexameters mentioning the Chian artists Mikkiadis and Archermos, known also from literary sources. The Nike, nevertheless, does come from some island workshop, possibly of Chios. About 540 B.C.

10,11. These two kouroi 10 and 11 are members of the number of excellent works found in the sanctuary of Apollo on Mt. Ptoon. They are the work of some artist from one of the Aegean islands, possibly Naxos. About 580 B.C.

3858. Although found at Moschato near Athens, this kouros, too, is the work of an artist from Naxos. About 580 B.C.

1558. The kouroi of Dipylon, Sounion and Merenda reflect the Attic concept of the plastic representation of the young male — the "andropais". This kouros from Melos (about the middle of the 6th century B.C.) transfers us to the Aegean world with its delicate and graceful proportions. These features can be seen in many works of that period and witness the presence of an important local art school.

1586. Head of kouros, from Melos, middle 6th century B.C.

Room 10, of the Kouros of Volomandra

1906. Coming from the grave of a young man in Volomandra, Attica, this kouros (middle 6th century B.C.) is unlike the other Attic kouroi. Made of Paros marble, it shows, despite some imperfections, a very careful execution of the head: there is a pronounced smile and a delicate rendering of facial features. The hair falls about the forehead crowning it with meshes that have been likened to flames. The body, too, is markedly different. While in the kouroi seen earlier most anatomical details were indicated by grooves and nervures, the representation of the musculature and the transitions from one level to another show here considerable technical and artistic improvement. The body has plasticity and richness.

38. The fragment of a memorial stele depicting the head of a smiling young man comes from Dipylon near Kerameikos (about 560 B.C.). A round discus (held up by the left hand) is visible behind the head. The hair, gathered together and tied low at the back of the head enhances the perfection of the chiselled features. Its maker was the same artist who created the horse-rider No 590 of the Acropolis (the head, known as "Rampin" is in the Louvre). Imagine the stele painted in vivid colours as was the ancients' custom.

2687. Following the Persian Wars, the Athenians, prompted by Themistocles, hurriedly built a wall to protect Athens. Thucydides tells us that even steles from graves were used as building material, like this stele from the wall at Kerameikos. To facilitate construction, the largest part of the relief was carved off. The stele shows a young man holding a spear. In the lower part, a running Gorgon wears a belted chiton richly decorated with spirals and meanders in relief. Its presence on the stele seems to have been apotropaic or even intended to inspire fear. About 560 B.C.

Earlier archaic Attic steles were often decorated with an all round carved Sphinx on top — a common theme in Egyptian sculpture. The Sphinx is also used as a decorative design in orientally influenced Greek pottery. The presence of the Sphinx in Greek memorial steles has no symbolic significance. As shown by a grave inscription of the 6th century B.C. from Thessaly, the Sphinx was meant merely as a guardian of tombs.

28. Well preserved Sphinx from Spata, Attica, which served as the top of a stele. The wings on the chest are depicted schematically. The "polos" on the head was originally ornamented with painted on rosettes. There is a necklace around the neck. The rear side of the statue has not been worked by the sculptor. About 570 B.C.

2891. This Sphinx comes from·Themistocles' wall·in Athens (see No 2687). The upper part of the wings was found at Kerameikos. Details, such as the wings, were indicated by colour painting which has been preserved in some places. About 550 B.C.

45

44. *Kouros No 1906 from Volomandra, Attica.*

45. *Statue of seated goddess No 2569 from the sanctuary of Nemesis in Ramnous, Attica.*

46. *Fragment of a funerary stele No 38 showing the head of a young man and the discus he held over his head, from Dipylon.*

47. *Relief stele No 1959 depicting a naked warrior, from Athens.*

47

Room 11, of Aristion

29. Few memorial steles are so famous as the stele of Aristion (late 6th century B.C.) found at Velanidesa, Attica in 1838. It was at first regarded, wrongly of course, as coming from the grave of a warrior who fell at the battle of Marathon. Aristion is shown in the dress of an Athenian hoplite: he wears a clinging short chiton, an armour covering the trunk and jambs protecting the legs, while the feet from the ankles down are bare; the raised left arm holds a spear. If one looks carefully, one discerns the painted designs that used to adorn the armour at the shoulders, chest and waist. The finely rendered folds of the cloth on the thighs and arms are a realistic addition to the perfect moulding of the bare flesh. Justly proud of his achievement, the sculptor stated his name in an inscription engraved in the narrow strip on which rest the feet of the deceased's figure: «ἔργον Ἀριστοκλέος» (work of Aristokles); on the front side of the rectangular base supporting the stele, the name of the deceased is mentioned in the customary possessive form: Aristion's. The stele was painted in vivid colours: red in the background of the relief, and in the hair, beard and lips, blue for the helmet and the armour. The upper part of the helmet, the plume, is missing and so is the top (crown) of the stele, probably an anthemion with lateral helices.

41. While Aristion's stele is the triumph of mature archaic sculpture, this "epicranon" (about 550 B.C.) from Lambres (present-day Lambrica) of Attica, corresponds to an earlier stage of the art. The scene depicted on the front side (was the deceased a cavalry man?) including two horses, two shields and a spear, a mourning man and woman on one narrow side and a mourning man (the father?) on the other, is in imprinted relief, and the contours are stressed by engraved lines. The decoration is also engraved: there are rosettes on the abacus, tongues in the cavity between the abacus and the representation. At the edges to the right and left of the horseman, there are "plochmoi". This "epicranon" must have stood on the tall and slender stele of the deceased and was probably topped by an all round carved Sphinx.

3686. This kouros comes from the small island of Kea (about 530 B.C.) and is somewhat later than the kouros of Volomandra we saw earlier. The body is different in that it is the body of a fully grown man though the slightly smiling face is youthful. The chest, the abdomen and the thighs are powerful, in contrast with the immature body of the kouros of Volomandra.

3072. An object of interest with regard to ancient religious practice is the marble mask of Dionysos (about 520 B.C.) found in the sanctuary of that god at Ikaria, Attica. Suspended from a tree over a set of actual clothes representing the body, it served as the ceremonial likeness of Dionysos Dendrites.

81. The artists of the archaic period attached great importance to the inscriptions that accompanied their works - witness the careful lettering on this base, which supported the statue of a young woman, "kore", (the beautifully shaped toes and parts of the sandals are preserved). The inscription states that the statue was erected on the girl's grave by the care of her father, and it also mentions the sculptor's name, Phaedimos: αϜυτάρ: Φαίδιμος: ἐργάσατο (Phaedimos chiselled this). This Phaedimos, a sculptor of the 6th c., is known from several statue bases. About 550 B.C.

30. Memorial stele of Lyseus, with a painted on representation of a standing man wearing a chiton, himation and sandals, looking to the right. In his right hand he held a vase (*cantharus*), the raised left hand held perhaps laurel leaves. Below this scene there was a naked male figure on horseback. Preserved at the base of the stele is the engraved inscription: *"Λυσέαι ἐνθάδε σεμα πατὲρ Σέμον ἐπέθεκεν".* (Here the stele of Lyseas father Semon dedicated). This stele was found near the site of the stele of Aristion (No 29) at Velanideza, Attica, in 1838.

93. Disc of Paros marble, 0,27 diameter, which bore the painted likeness of a sitting bearded man looking to the right. Above this is a circular incription saying: *"μνέμα τόδ' Αἰνέο σοφίας ἰατρο ἀρίστο"* (this is the grave of the wise and excellent physician Aeneias). From ancient sources, it is known that this physician Aeneias was connected with the great Hippocrates. The shape of a disc is unusual in tomb monuments. We have a limited number of discs from Attica of approximately the same shape and size, apparently connected with the dead, but their precise significance is unknown. About 500 B.C.

Room 12, of the "hoplitodromos"

1959. The figure of this naked young man is alive with movement (late 6th c. B.C.). It is commonly referred to as the "hoplitodromos" (hoplite race runner) and it has also been thought to represent Pheidippides, the Marathon runner. According to the prevailing contemporary view, however, the young man is not running but performing a war dance known as "phyrrychios". A noteworthy feature of this relief is the orientation of the body: the upper part is shown in front view, the head and the lower part of the body are lateral, but opposite, views. This conventional solution in the presentation of the whole male body is also seen in other works of the archaic period.

1933-1938. The temple of Aphaea in Aegina was decorated on both its pediments with carved scenes showing the campaign of Herakles against Troy (eastern pediment), and the campaign of Agamemnon also against Troy (western pediment). The statues composing these scenes were found in 1811 during excavations carried out by Cockerell and others at the temple of Aphaea and now adorn the collection of sculptures of the Munich Museum. Other excavations, in 1903, led to the discovery of the relics of the sculptures from an earlier sculptural decoration of the eastern pediment. This had been taken down and replaced for unknown reasons, possibly as a result of damage done by the Persians in 480 B.C. From this earlier eastern pediment (500-490 B.C.) come the six warrior heads - worthy examples of the famous sculptural art of Aegina, whose most celebrated representative was Onatas.

3711. Statue of a sitting god, possibly Zeus or Dionysos, from Athens. About 500 B.C.

782. Crown of a tomb stele from Kerameikos, preserving some of its ancient colouring. Late 6th century B.C.

3370. Trunk of a kouros from Attica. Late 6th century B.C.

4797. This archaic Ionic capital was found in the church of the prophet Elia in the village Sykamino of Attica, and it may have served as a base for a sphinx. On one side, the helices coming out of the echinus, the round part of the capital resting on the column, are concave, on the other side they are convex - a feature found in several archaic works. Fanning out between the helices are engraved golden leaves. There is no certainty that this capital is of Attic origin.

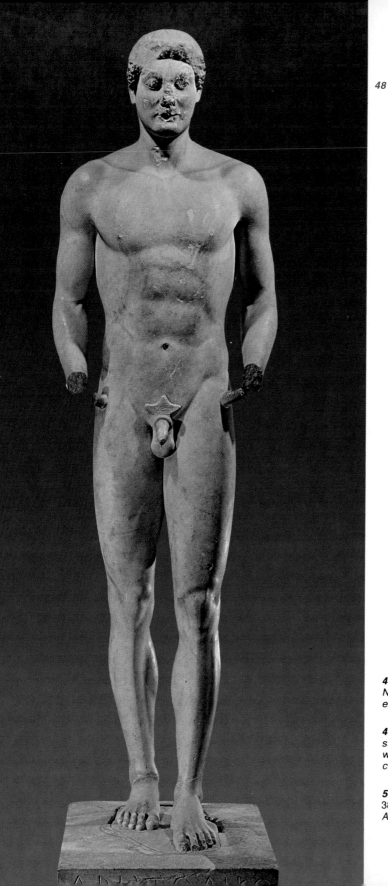

48. The kouros Aristodikos No 3938 from Attica, a fine example of Attic plastic art.

49. The celebrated funerary stele of Artistion No 29, a work of the sculptor Aristocles.

50. The kouros Croesus No 3851 from Anavyssos, Attica.

Room 13, of Aristodikos

3938. This kouros represents the mature period of archaic Attic sculpture. It is the likeness of a young man belonging to a wealthy aristocratic family of Attica, as can be inferred from the fact that such a statue was erected on his grave.

His name - *Aristodikos* - is shown on the base. According to the interpreter of the work Chr. Carousos, the unknown sculptor probably learned his art in the workshop that produced the marbles of the temple of Athena Polias on the Acropolis and may also be the author of kore No 623 of the Acropolis. About 500 B.C.

3851. The exquisite kouros Croesus (about 520 B.C.) comes from Anavyssos and he ended up in the National Museum after many adventures. A largely intact work with only minor defects, it shows the high quality of Attic art in that period. An elegy engraved on the base informs us that Croesus died in battle" στε̄θε καὶ οἴκτιρον Κροίσο παρὰ σε̄μα θανόντος / hòν ποτ' ἐνὶ προμάχοις ὄλεσε θο̄ρος "Αρες" (stand near this stele and mourn for Croesus who was killed by ferocious Ares (Mars) while fighting in the first line).

2569. The small statue sitting in a diphros and found at the temple of Nemesis in Ramnous, Attica (about 520 B.C.) is the likeness of some goddess, dedicated to the stern mistress of the sanctuary. Dressed in Ionic chiton and himation, it is both graceful and dignified.

3476. This base of a kouros from the cemetery of Kerameikos (about 510 B.C.) is unique for its illustrative decoration, in relief, with themes taken from the life of the young Athenians in the gymnasium. On the front side there are in the middle two wrestling adolescents, another, to the left, is preparing to jump, and a fourth adolescent, to the right, is drawing a line on the ground. On the left side of the base six other youths are shown either as competitors or as spectators (the two at the right extremity). On the right side of the base, the young boys in the gymnasium are having fun. Dressed in the himation, the two boys in the middle are trying to cause a dog and a cat to fight, while two others, one behind each of the central figures, are watching the amusing scene.

Painted in vivid colours, and skilfully carved in bas relief, these scenes would remind visitors to the grave of the lost youth of the adolescent buried there. But there is no trace of sadness in these pictures of everyday life, which show an important aspect of the Athenian educational system.

Room 14, of the "Self-Crowned Athlete"

3344. An offering to Athena at her sanctuary in Sounion, this relief shows a naked young athlete, turning to the left while he crowns himself (about 460 B.C.). From the metal crown that adorned his head, only the holes that served to fasten it now remain. The blue background showing around the young man's body enhanced the bas relief and created an illusion of depth. The body appears to be rising out of the slab, as the right side is depicted in almost linear design. The stance and the expression of the young athlete show clearly that this was a pious offering to the great goddess.

3990. This round marble disc, now with a part missing, comes from the island of Melos, one of the Cyclades. Shown in relief is the head of a goddess, possibly of Aphrodite (about 460 B.C.). The hair was restrained by the "sack" at the back of the head, and the hole beside the ear indicates that it was tied with a, probably golden,

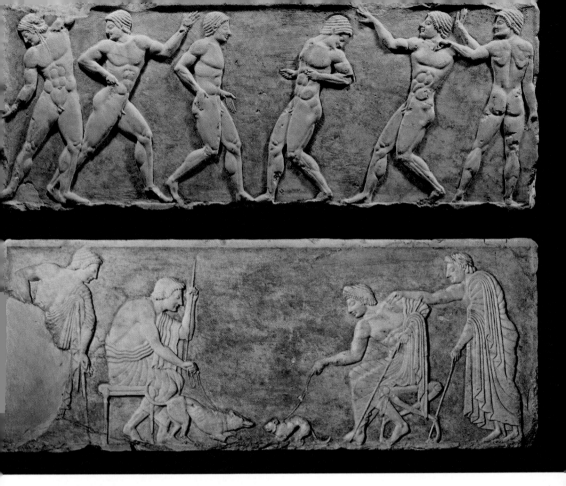

51. *Two aspects of the base of a kouros No 3476 from Kerameikos, with relief representations from the life of Athenian youths in the gymnasia. In the upper scene, 6 young men are training or watching others training. In the lower scene, young men amuse themselves watching a fight between a dog and a cat.*

band. In spite of the damaged surface of the marble, the work retains all its beauty as conceived by the islander who made it - probably an artist from Paros.

39. The memorial stele made by the sculptor Alxenor from Naxos (early 5th century B.C.) for the grave of a Boeotian in Orchomenos, where it was found, is typical of the freedom the Greeks felt in representing the dead. In this case the deceased, a bearded man wearing a himation, is offering his dog a grasshopper which he holds in his right hand. The inscription in hexameters, having the stele speak in the first person, is interesting: "'Αλξήνωρ μ' ἐποίησεν ὁ Νάξιος ἀλλ' ἐσίδεσθε". (Alxenor the Naxian made me but look). Despite some weaknesses, mainly due to the artist's effort to squeeze the scene into the narrow confines of the stele, this is a charming and typical example of insular-Ionic sculpture.

739. The funeral stele of Amphotto (about 440 B.C.) found near Thebes, bears witness to the skill of the unknown Boeotian sculptor who made it. The dead woman, wearing a veil belted at the waist and a "polos" on the head, is goddess-like. Engraved to the left of her face is the name Amphotto.

53

52

52. Round marble disc No 3990 from Melos, showing in relief the head of a goddess, perhaps Aphrodite.

53. Funerary stele No 39 from Orchomenos, a work of the sculptor Alxenor from Naxos.

54. Votive relief No 3344, the so-called "self-crowning man" from the sanctuary of Athena at Sounion.

55. *The excellent bronze statue No 15161 of Poseidon found in the sea off cap Artemision in Euboea.*

4778, 4779. Two Ionic capitals from the temple of Athena in Sounion. There was a sanctuary of that goddess near the sanctuary of Poseidon, and two temples were built in it, the earlier including an external Ionic colonnade. In the Roman period, most of the parts of that temple were transferred to the Agora in Athens, where the temple was to be rebuilt. A third capital and some other pieces of the temple of Athena are indeed still to be found in the Agora. In the antiquity, these capitals were brightly coloured and had painted decorations of egg, lance, and meander designs; in other capitals of the same style, these ornamental designs are in relief. Later half of 5th century B.C.

Room 15, of Poseidon

15161. Fishermen from Skiathos fishing off cape Artemission in Euboea, found the left arm of this statue in 1926 and the rest of the statue in 1928. There can be little doubt that the Poseidon was part of a cargo, probably on its way to Rome, when the ship carrying it sank. The statue is typical of the ancients' idea of what a god looked like and what constituted the beauty of a male body. With legs apart and the left foot bearing his weight, the god spreads out his arms and hurls the trident with his right. The hair is tied around the head, while the forehead is casually covered with small locks. The sculptor is unknown. From the beginning, similarities in style were identified between this and the "Apollo of Omphalos" (No 45), also in this room, which is attributed, but again without certainty, to the great sculptor of the 5th century Kalamis. Some works of Kalamis and descriptions of the main features of his work can be found in ancient writers, and the Poseidon does indeed demonstrate these features. But whether it is the work of Kalamis or not, it is certainly the work of a great artist. About 460 B.C.

126. This large scene in relief (440-430 B.C.) shows the goddess Demeter holding a sceptre on the right, her daughter Persephone holding a torch on the left, and in the middle turned to the left, Triptolemos with just a himation thrown over his naked body. From mythology we know that Triptolemos, travelling round the world, taught men the cultivation of wheat. The relief shows the moment when Demeter hands over to him the ears of wheat - they were probably of gold - while Persephone blesses him. The contrast between the three figures is striking. Demeter wears a woollen Doric chiton, a heavy and austere garment forming straight folds; Persephone, the younger woman, is dressed with a variously draped Ionic chiton. It was noted as soon as this work was found that the two figures probably reflected conventional likenesses used in the cult of these goddesses: Demeter old-fashioned and austere, the daughter more elegant and fashionable. Triptolemos, smaller in size, expresses pious devotion. All three figures, however, contribute with their stance and their expression to the creation of an atmosphere of mystical exaltation.

45. This statue is known as "Apollo of the omphalos" because it was in its vicinity that the base with the omphalos No 46 (to be seen a little later in this room) was found in the theatre of Dionysos in 1862. The statue portrays the god Apollo, with hair casually falling on his forehead and a braid around the head. It is one of several copies produced in the 2nd century A.D., of an important work of the middle of the 5th century B.C., possibly a statue of Apollo Alexikakos by Kalamis. Kalamis was a representative of the transitional period in sculpture and was noted for the gracefulness and delicacy rather than for the originality of his work.

56. Large ceremonial relief No 126 from the sanctuary of Demeter in Eleusis, showing Demeter, Triptolemos and Persephone.

57. The "Apollo of Omphalos" No 45, from the theatre of Dionysus, possibly a work of the sculptor Kalamis.

Room 16, of Myrrina

Attic sepulchral monuments: In the Room of Mycenae we saw some of the steles from the Mycenaean tomb circles A and B. This ancient custom of "marking" graves found its highest expression in Attica.

In the first rooms of sculptures, several kouroi including the kouros of Dipylon, Aristodikos, Croesus, as well as the kore on the tomb of Phrasikleia, are tomb statues. During the same period, a stele could be used for the same purpose instead of a statue. Like the steles of Alxenor or Aristion, these were usually tall upright slabs showing one figure on their long and narrow surface. On the more rarely used larger steles, a number of persons were sometimes shown.

From a text of the orator Cicero, we know that in the 6th century B.C., an Athenian law prohibited the construction of sumptuous tomb monuments and even prescribed the maximum expenditure allowed for this purpose. This law put a temporary stop to the flourishing memorial art, and has no doubt deprived us of many a fine work of art.

This was followed by a lengthy gap, and only around the middle of the 5th century B.C. did sculptured gravestones again appear on the graves of Attica. From then on to the end of the 4th century B.C., the profusion of steles has formed a unique series in ancient art.

Apart from the steles which were the main type of grave ornament, some other kinds of monuments were used. These included marble urns, which could be in the shape of a lekythos like that of Myrrina No 4485 or a "loutrophoros", though the latter type was reserved for the graves of unmarried persons. Round carved lions were common and even dogs are sometimes seen.

Following its reappearance in the 5th century, the grave stele evolved not only in style according to the artistic tendencies of the time, but also in morphology. The simple relief of the 5th century was soon surrounded with structural elements such as posts and pediments, the relief became higher and higher until it approached all-round sculpture towards the end of the 4th century, as is the case with the monument of Aristonautes. Steles are now placed in temple replicas of which many have astonishing dimensions. Similar changes occured in the construction of the actual graves. The earlier simple mounds grew into large edifices destined to receive the dead of a family for many generations. The extravagant indulgence in ostentation, especially marked in grave monuments, was again checked by Demetrius of Phaleron who, with the support of Cassandros, king of Macedonia, ruled Athens as an absolute monarch from 317 to 307. He enacted a law against excessive luxury, under which magnificent sepulchral monuments were prohibited and grave ornaments were restricted to the stele, the small column and the flat gravestone. This may have been a morally and socially justified measure, but in terms of art one can only regret the many more exquisite works which, to judge by the impetus of monumental art at the end of the 4th century, would certainly have come into being.

4485. Funeral marble vessel (*lekythos*) with a representation in relief. On the right, the dead woman - her name is Myrrina as mentioned in the inscription over her head - is being led to Hades by Hermes Psychopompos (conductor of souls) who is to her right. Hermes, in a characteristic movement, takes hold of her hand, while her stance, her covered and lowered head, is suggestive of her terrible fate. On the left side of the picture, three smaller-sized men, the last one leaning on a post, watch the scene. Hermes is wearing the winged sandals indicative of his other capacity, that of messenger of the gods. "Messenger of the immortals" is the name attributed to him

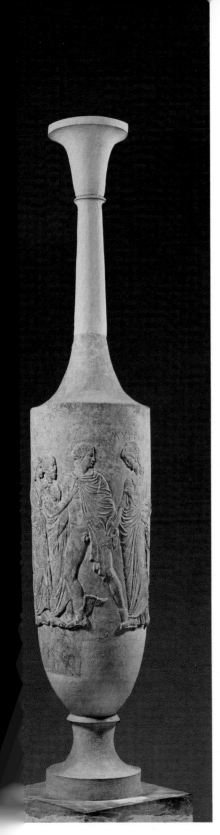

58. The burial lekythos of Myrinna No 4485 from Athens.

59. Funerary stele No 3845 of Mnesagora and her brother Nikohares; erected on their grave by their parents according to an epigram engraved on the epistyle; abt. 440 B.C.

60. Fine funerary stele No 715 from Salamis or Aegina.

in the Homeric hymn in his honour and in a votive offering by the military chief Kallimachos. About 420 B.C.

715. This is the larger part of a stele from Salamis or Aegina. Shown in relief is the likeness of a youth who stands turning to the left. In his raised right hand, he holds a cage; below the cage and on top of a column, there is a cat. Standing disconsolately before the column is the youth's child-slave. One authority in ancient Greek art considered this to be a work of Pheidias' disciple Agorakritos, but this seems to have been a wrong assumption and that the work must be assigned to the insular-Ionic area. On top of the stele, on the front side of the cornice, there are anthemia and lotus-flowers in relief. About 430 B.C.

Room 17, of Ramnous

At the NE extremity of Attica, on the coast of the southern Euboic Gulf, there was the ancient city of Ramnous, whose ruins cover a large area. At the centre of these ruins is the sanctuary of Nemesis, including two temples. The smaller of the two dates from the end of the 6th century B.C., the other dates from the later half of the 5th century and was built by the "architect of the Theseion", whose other works include the temple of Poseidon in Sounion, the temple of Hephaestos (Theseion) in the Agora of Athens, and the temple of Ares at Acharnae. In the temple of Nemesis, there was a statue of that goddess, made by Agorakritos, a disciple of Pheidias. The base of the statue was decorated with representations in relief, relics of which can

61. *Bilateral votive relief No 1783 from Phaleron depicting Echelos, Basile and Hermes on one side, Artemis, three nymphs and Kephisos on the other.*

62. *Statue of a young man No 199 with its ancient inscribed base, dedicated to Nemesis in her sanctuary at Ramnous, Attica, a work of Lysikleides.*

ɔe seen in this room. Sculpture No 2348 is believed to have been part of the acroterium of the larger temple.

2348. Remains from a large-size sculpture believed to have been an acroterium of the great temple of Nemesis at Ramnous, Attica, and attributed to the disciple of Pheidias, Agorakritos. It depicted the abduction of Oreithyia by Boreas. About 420 B.C.

1783. Votive relief with representations on both sides. On one side, shown in a chariot drawn by four horses are Echelos, a chthonian hero, and the nymph Basile, an also chthonian deity. Hermes as "bride-leader" is driving the chariot. The other side pictures Artemis, three nymphs and the river Kephissos (in whose estuary at Phaleron the statue was found) with horns on his head. On the cornice, one side is inscribed: "To Hermes and to the Nymphs" indicating the deities to whom the offering was dedicated, and the other bears the names: Hermes, Echelos, Basile, identifying the persons in the quadriga. The relief, which is important in more ways than one, dates from about 410 B.C. The actual base of the relief is in the Altar Room and bears the following votive incription: *"Κηφισόδοτος Δεμογένος / Βουτάδης ἰδρύσατο / καὶ τὸν βωμόν"* (Kephisodotos of Demogenes, Boutades, dedicated the altar).

199. This statue of a young man standing on the original pedestal, also comes from the celebrated sanctuary of Ramnous, Attica. It is considered to belong to the school of Agorakritos, the disciple of the great Pheidias, and was dedicated by

Lisikleides, son of Epandrides, whose likeness the statue probably is. On the dark marble pedestal, there is a beautifully engraved inscription, interesting in its simplicity: "Λυσικλείδης ἀνέθηκ/εν 'Επανδρίδο ὑὸς ἀπη/αρχὴν τόνδε θεᾶι τῆι/δε ἥ τόδ' ἔχει τέμενος". About 420 B.C.

Showcase: The small sculptures in the showcase are relics of the figures in relief which decorated three sides of the pedestal of the statue of Nemesis at Ramnous, Attica. According to the traveller Pausanias, who had seen it, the base represented Helen being introduced by her adoptive mother Leda to her real mother Nemesis, the mistress of the sanctuary. The base with the reliefs was made by the sculptor Agorakritos, or at least in his workshop, at the same time as the statue of Nemesis, which is known to have been a work by his own hand. About 420 B.C.

1500. This is an important relief from Piraeus. On the right, Dionysos reclines on a couch, holding a flask in his left hand and a rhyton in his right. A woman is seated on the edge of the couch at the feet of Dionysos. Approaching the god are three men in the attire of actors: the first on the left, whose face was added on or, perhaps, was an actual mask and has been lost, is holding a drum, the second has a drum in one hand and an old man's mask in the other, the third standing before the woman in the attitude of a supplicant has in his left hand a tragic mask, probably also of an old man. All three actors wear long belted chitons. Some investigators have associated this relief with Euripides' "Bacchae". Late 5th century B.C.

1391. Dedicated by a winner of the "apovasis" competition in the great games held every four years at Amphiareio of Oropos, this relief shows the rear side of a quadriga with the charioteer and the jumper. The front part showing the four horses drawing the chariot has been lost. The charioteer bends slightly forward as he holds the reins and drives the horses, the jumper is naked but for his helmet and his shield - according to the regulations of this competition. He still holds onto the chariot with his right hand but is about to jump. This relief, and another with the same theme which is now in Berlin, are the earliest evidence of games being held at Amphiareio. On the abacus, over the representation, the inscription "[...]εος ἐγγύην" is visible. Late 5th c. B.C.

226. Ancient works of art associated with historical persons known from literary sources are, understandably, particularly interesting. This is the case with this relief, found during excavations conducted by the French School of Archaeology under G. Fougeres at Mantineia in 1887. On the right-hand side of this only partly preserved relief, there is a headless standing woman dressed in a veil of the style customary in Argos. In her left hand, she holds the liver of an animal which, as we know from literary sources, was used in divination. In the lower right-hand side, part of the trunk of a palm-tree, a tree sacred to Apollo, can be seen. According to prevailing, and unchallenged, opinion, the woman depicted in the relief is no other than the famous soothsayer Diotima, a priestess in Mantineia, whose idea of love (i.e. the Platonic idea of love) is discussed by Socrates in Plato's "Symposium". The "Symposium" is the source from which Diotima is known, and although we have no confirmation of her existence from other sources, it is generally believed that this woman who "revealed the nature of love" to Socrates, was a historical person. About 410 B.C.

Sculptures from the Heraeon of Argos: As we know from the historian Thucydides and the traveller Pausanias, the temple of Hera in her sanctuary near Argos was burned in 423 B.C. as a result of the carelessness of the priestess Chrysis.

63. Small head of Dioscuros No 4932 from the relief decoration of the base of a statue of Nemesis from Ramnous, Attica.

64. Funerary stele No 226 from Mantineia; it is thought to portray the woman diviner Diotima known from Plato's Symposion.

63

A new temple was built between 423 and 416 B.C. and ornamented with sculptures on the pediments and metopes. It also included a gold and ivory ceremonial statue of the goddess, made by Polykleitos. According to Pausanias' account, the sculptures on the pediments showed the birth of Zeus and the Gigantomachy, and the war and capture of Troy, respectively. It seems, however, that in his description of the pediments, Pausanias included the metopes, because those found do indeed show a gigantomachy and various war scenes. Some other fragments of sculptures suggest scenes of the War of the Amazons. The sculptures in this room are parts of the decoration of the temple of Hera: No **3869,** trunk of female statuette, possibly from the western pediment; Nos **1572-1573,** trunks of warriors; No **1574,** trunk of an Amazon; No **3500,** metope of the temple showing a Greek and an Amazon in combat; No **1563,** head of warrior; No **1564,** head of Amazon wearing a Phrygian hat; Nos **1581-82,** parts of the sculptured sima of the temple of Hera: impressive lion-heads, through whose mouths rainwater drained from the roofs, are surrounded by anthemions and lotus-flowers projected out of helices. Cuckoo birds stand on small helices. This bird is associated with Hera: as Pausanias tells the story, when Zeus courted Hera, he assumed the form of a cuckoo that Hera chased in play.

65. *Marble head No 1571 from the ceremonial statue of Hera, from that goddesse's sanctuary near Argos.*

66. *The famous "Athena of Varvakion" No 129, a Roman copy of the gold- and - ivory ceremonial statue of the goddess by Pheidias, which stood at the Parthenon of the Acropolis of Athens.*

1571. This excellent head of Hera comes from a ceremonial statue in her sanctuary. Its majestic expression, as rendered by the Argive sculptor of the school of Polykleitos who made it, gives us an idea of how the ancients imagined the great Olympian goddess. The hair is tied with a wide band, its loose ends falling at the back. About 420 B.C.

Rooms 19 and 20, of Athena of Varvakeion

Displayed in these two contiguous rooms are sculptures, round or in relief, of the 5th and 4th centuries or copies of celebrated works of that period. Many of them deserve attention e.g.: the relief dedicated by Archandros to the Nymphs (No **1329**, about 410 B.C.) with an engraved inscription to that effect: *"Αρχανδρος Νύμφαισιν ἀ[νέθηκεν]*. (Archandros dedicated to the Nymphs): the fragment of a votive relief representing Persephone and Demeter (No **3572**, about 420 B.C.); the temple-shaped relief showing Apollo, Leto and Artemis (No **1389**, about 410 B.C.). The male trunk **1612** is a Roman copy of a statue of Apollo known from its most famous copy as "Apollo of Kassel". The original is believed to have been "Apollo

Parnopios" by Pheidias. Also copies of works by Pheidias are the statuette of Athena No **3000,** and the larger-than-life head No **3718** known as "Athena of Pnyx" from the site where it was found in 1931. This copy of the 2nd century A.D. is lifeless, retaining nothing of the great art of Pheidias.

129. The most renowned work of the great sculptor Pheidias was perhaps the gold and ivory statue of Athena in the Parthenon. The marble copy No **129** known as "Athena of Varvakeion", 1/12 the size of the original, represents the external appearance of that statue, but completely lacks its art and spirit. Nevertheless, this 2nd or 3rd century A.D. copy is valuable as a source of information about Pheidias' Virgin Athena.

The fullest description of the then already famous statue is given by Pausanias, who saw it in the Parthenon: "The statue itself is made of ivory and gold. The helmet is decorated with a sphinx on the top and with griffins in relief on the sides. The statue represents Athena standing in a chiton reaching down to her feet. On the chest, there is an ivory Medusa in relief. The goddess holds an approximately four cubit high Nike and has a spear in the other hand.

At her feet there is a shield, and near the spear there is a serpent which must be representing Erichthonios. Pictured in relief on the pedestal of the statue is the birth of Pandora". Additional information is provided by other authors. Pliny says that on the convex side of the shield there was an Amazonomachy in relief, and on the concave side a battle between Lapiths and Centaurs. From Plutarch's biography of Pericles we learn that in the Amazonomachy on the shield, "Pheidias portrayed himself as an aged bald man lifting a rock with both hands, and Pericles in an admirable likeness fighting with an Amazon". According to Aristotle, the statue had a hidden mechanism that would cause it to fall apart if the attempt was made to remove any one of its parts.

Room 18, of Hegeso

3624. Sepulchral stele with relief decoration of the Athenian woman Hegeso. The young woman is shown seated and looking at some jewel she has just taken out of a box held open over her lap by a slave-girl standing in front of her. There is an admirably harmonious contrast between the mistress and the slave. The former, sitting on an elegant chair (*klismos*) wears a chiton and himation whose folds allow the lines of the body to be sketched, while the slave wears a long-sleeved chiton, its straight folds covering with restrained grace the figure of the young girl. The stele, made around 410 B.C., is an excellent work of art, ascribed to one of the great sculptors of the 5th century; it is also interesting in that it expresses the idea of that particular period concerning the manifestations of sorrow. The dead woman's name - Hegeso Proxeno - is engraved over the scene.

765. Stele showing a seated woman holding a mirror on the left, and a man standing before her on the right, to whom she seems to be saying farewell. Their names - Mika, Dion - are engraved on the epistyle. About 430 B.C.

778. Stele of Euembolos from Piraeus. The man is shown seated, holding two birds - one in each hand - offering them to two children standing in front of him. His name is engraved under the "kymation": *Εὐέμπολος*. Late 5th century B.C.

718. Stele from Piraeus showing a standing woman dressed in chiton and himation which covers the head. Kneeling in front of her, a servant is helping her put

68

67. The famous funerary stele of Hegeso Proxenos No 3624 from Kerameikos, abt. 410 B.C.

68. Bronze statue of a horse with the little rider No 15177 from the shipwreck of Artemision.

69. *Female statue No 1827 of the "Herakleion girl" type, 2nd c. B.C. copy of a celebrated earlier original of the late 4th c. B.C., from Delos.*

70. *Statue no 242 of the "Herakleion woman" type, from Aegion.*

71. *Copy of the statue of the "diadem-bearer" (diadoumenos) of Polykleitos No 1826 from Delos.*

on her sandal, as though she were going for a walk, according to one observer. Another woman standing by her side, holds the dead girl's jewel-box. Engraved on the horizontal band of the pediment is the inscription: Ameinokleia, daughter of Andromenos. Late 4th century.

939. Simple stele from Piraeus; the upper part is decorated with anthemion, helices and acanthus between anthemion halves. Below the kymation is engraved the name of the dead: Nausikrates son of Socrates Agnousios. First half of 4th c. B.C.

754. Crown of sepulchral monument erected by the city of Athens in the public "sema" in honour of the Athenian cavalry men who fell at the battle of Corinth in July and in the battle of Coroneia in August of 394 B.C. The complete monument was seen by the traveller Pausanias when he visited Athens in the 2nd c. A.D. The part which has been preserved is ornamented with rich vegetal decorative designs. There is an anthemion in the middle, with flowers, helices and rosettes on the right and left. Anthemion halves decorate the edges. The band below bears an engraved inscription mentioning the names of the dead.

The man Dexileos mentioned among the dead is the 20-year-old youth from Thorikon, Attica, whose parents erected over the family grave the exquisite relief now kept in the museum of Kerameikos.

2744. There was a second monument erected by the city of Athens in honour of the dead of the battles of Corinth and Coroneia in 394 B.C., and it is from that monument that we have this slab showing in relief: a standing hoplite on the left, a mounted horseman on a galloping horse, and between them a naked hoplite lying on the ground. Preserved in part below the scene is the inscription engraved by the city to perpetuate the memory of her fallen sons: *"['Αθηναίων οἵδε ἀπέθα]νον ἐν Κορίνθωι καί ἐμ Βοιωτοῖ[ς]" (These Athenians died in Corinth and Boeotia)*. This was followed by the names of the 10 Athenian fractions and below each of those the names of its dead.

The funeral and burial of the dead of war took place in Athens at public expense and "everyone wishing to do so, both citizens and aliens" were allowed to follow the procession. Even the female relatives of the dead had access to the place of burial, where they would gather in lamentation. The urns were placed in the public monument in the loveliest suburb of Athens, where all those fallen in battle were buried except the dead of Marathon" (Thucydides).

Room 21, of "Diadoumenos"

1826. The statue of the young man known as "Diadoumenos" was found in Delos. It is a copy dating from the 1st century B.C., of a famous and popular work of the 5th century B.C. by the Argive sculptor Polykleitos, also the author of that other famous statue of the "Doryphoros" known as the "Canon". In describing the work, Pliny said that the young man represented by the statue, an athlete or a god, was tying his hair with a band. The "Diadoumenos" is a work of the mature period of Polykleitos (430-420 B.C.), which explains the soulfulness marking its features, as well as the influence of later Attic art.

ΤΗΛΕΦΑΝΗΣ ΝΙΚΗΡΑΤΟΣ ΔΗΜΟΦΙΛΟΣ
ΤΑΙΣ ΝΥΝΦΑΙΣ ΑΝΕΘΕΣΑΝ

72. *Marble plinth No 3614, possibly from a large grave monument of the late 4th century, with fragments of an Amazonomachy. In the middle of the representation, a naked warrior with shield and sword attacks an amazon who defends herself with a pelte; there is a second amazon to the right.* **73.** *Votive relief No 4466 from Penteli portraying three nymphs, Hermes and Pan.*

Polykleitos, Myron and Pheidias were the most famous sculptors of the fifth century B.C. According to ancient tradition all three were pupils of the sculptor Ageladas, who hailed from Argos. Though there is probably little truth in this claim, for chronological reasons, it nevertheless indicates the esteem in which he was held by the ancient Greeks.

15177. In addition to the bronze statue of Poseidon, the shipwreck of Artemision has also produced this galloping horse ridden by the little jockey. It is not absolutely certain that the two figures belonged together in the way they are combined here. This can only be ascertained by further study. The horse, every part of its body straining, seems to be making an ultimate effort in its headlong rush and a similar strain can be seen in the body of the little rider (middle 2nd century B.C.).

3622. "The Great Herculean", the name by which this statue is known, relates to the "Little Herculean", No 1827. The two statues are so called because they are similar in style to two statues found in the Herculanum of Italy, now in the Museum in Dresden. The original models, representing Demeter and Persephone according to one opinion, were made in the workshop of Praxiteles. The types of the two statues were widespread in antiquity and were used by sculptors in portraits and memorial monuments for hundreds of years.

74. *Statue of a flying Nike No 159 from the temple of Artemis in the sanctuary of Asklepios at Epidaurus.*

75. *Acroterium of the temple of Asklepios at Epidaurus No 157, depicting a woman, perhaps a Nereid or Aura on a horse coming out of the Ocean.*

Room 34, of the altar

1495. This monolithic marble altar stands on a foundation forming three steps. The narrow sides rise and curve out as in the Ionic capitals, and are decorated with helices. From the inscription engraved on one side we learn that the altar was dedicated by the Athenian parliament to Aphrodite Hegemone and the Graces when the archon of Athens was Dionysius in the early 2nd century B.C.: "Ἡ βουλὴ ἡ ἐπὶ Διονυσίου ἄρχοντος ἀνέθηκεν Ἀφροδίτει Ἡγεμόνει τοῦ Δήμου καὶ Χάρισιν ἐπὶ ἱερέως Μικίωνος τοῦ Εὐρυκλείδου Κηφισιέως στρατηγοῦντος ἐπὶ τὴν παρασκευὴν Θεοβούλου τοῦ Θεοφάνους Πειραιέως".

4465a, 4466. These two reliefs were found in 1952 in a cave of Mt. Penteli, where the Nymphs were worshipped. The first, dating from about 360 B.C., shows three Nymphs, Hermes and Pan, and in front of them the three sponsors. Engraved on the pedestal is the votive inscription: "Dedicated to the Nymphs by Telephanes, Nikeratos and Demophilos". The second relief, later than the first by a few decades, is in the shape of a cave, in which are, from left to right, three Nymphs (one seated), Hermes, Pan (seated) and, towards the right end, the sponsor Agathemeros offering

a scarab to a naked young man who holds a wine-jug in his raised hand. On the marble base there is the inscription: ʼΑγαθήμερος Νύμφαις ἀνέθηκε *(Dedicated by Agathemeros to the Nymphs).*

Room 22, of Epidaurus

The great sanctuary of Asklepios at Epidaurus was excavated by the Greek archaeologist Panayotis Kavvadias, for the main part between the years 1882 and 1886. A large number of sculptures were found from the pediments of the god's great temple. The scene represented on the eastern pediment was the fall of Troy, and on the western pediment an Amazonomachy—two very popular and often recurring themes in ancient sculpture. But the four sculptors who worked on the pediments of the temple (we know three of their names: Timotheos, Ectoridas and Theo...), worked with gusto and artistic liberty and their sculptures are unconventional, and show originality in both conception and execution. Apart from works belonging to the temple of Asklepios (figures from the pediments and acroteria), this room also contains sculptures from the temple of Artemis at Epidaurus, reliefs and statues dedicated to Asklepios and some architectural members, a lion-head from the cave of the temple of Asklepios and part of the famous syma of the Tholos, i.e. the round building in the sanctuary of Epidaurus.

Room 23, gravestone reliefs of the 4th century B.C.

772. Stele of a priest from Myrrinous, Attica. The figure of the priest, surrounded by a rectangular frame, wears a floor-length chiton, the sacrificial knife — the mark of his calling — in his right hand. On the upper part of the stele there are anthemions in relief and the name of the dead: Simos of Myrrinous. First half of the 4th century B.C.

870. The theme of this relief, the "farewell stele", seems to have been popular, as it is found in several steles of the 4th century. The seated woman, an expression of suffering on her face, reaches out to the woman standing before her, as if trying to hold on to life. The girl on the left participates in the scene by her expression. Middle of 4th century B.C.

1022. Steles as large as this — 3,20 m — were uncommon. The plain body of the stele was crowned with the richly decorated anthemion and helices. On the surface of the stele itself, which was only decorated with two rosettes, the name of the deceased was engraved: *Δαισίας Εὐθίου Ἁλαιεύς.*. Later the names of his two sons, Euthias and Euthykritos, were added. In many steles of this type we find the engraved names of a family's successive generations. Middle of 4th century B.C.

869. Widely known for its artistic value, this stele is known as the "stele of Ilissos" from the place where it was found in 1874. It is the work of an important craftsman of the school of Skopa and is an eminent example of the artist's expression of the grief of the living at the death of a departed youth. Fallen asleep on the lower left part is the young slave of the dead and between the dead youth and his old father is the dog, his faithful hunting companion. About 340 B.C.

770. Part of a stele showing a lion looking to the right. Above this are two rosettes and higher still the engraved name of the dead: Leon of Sinope. Clearly, the likeness of the lion symbolizes the name of the deceased and, perhaps, also his braveness. First half of 4th century B.C.

Room 24, gravestone reliefs of the 4th century

749. The stele of Plangon from Oropos, depicts several personages. Plangon is shown in her mortal agony, supported in a half-lying posture by the servant on the right. Another woman, possibly the mother, on the left, is trying to help and standing off in a grief-stricken stance, is the father. It has been observed that this type of stele, a number of which have been found was usually reserved for women dying in childbirth. Engraved beneath the pediment is the inscription: *"Πλανγὼν Τολμίδου Πλαταϊκή, Τολμίδης Πλαταεύς".* Second half of 4th century B.C.

2574. The temple-like edifice marking the family grave of Alexos from Sounion, is a good example of that type of monument. The relief included several figures of which only one has been preserved. A post each on the right and left supported the heavy entablature, where the following names were engraved:

Alexos	Philoumene	Phanostrate	Stratocles
(son of)	(daughter of)		(son of)
Stratocles	Theoxenos		Alexos
of Sounion	of Marathon		of Sounion

In smaller monuments of this type, the horizontal structure was often of pedimental form. About 320 B.C.

3716. Stele of a woman. Christos Carousos, borrowing an expression from an epigram of the late 5th century, wrote about this stele: "Intact, it must have been an impressive monument, one shining in the distance". On the left, there is a girl, a servant with only the head and the right arm preserved, on the right another girl holding a pyxis and, in the middle, the dead woman dressed in a chiton that appears light and natural. The central figure in the scene is the seated woman. Made by an outstanding artist in about 380 B.C., (one of whose important earlier works is in the museum of Piraeus), this relief shows influences from the art of the late 5th century, particularly of the "thorakia" in the temple of Athena Nike. The central figure is indeed making the same gesture as Hera on the eastern pediment of the Parthenon: this gesture may have some particular significance and may be related to who the woman was in life.

Rooms 25-27, votive and decree reliefs

The so-called decree reliefs, a series of which we will see presently, are valuable in the sense that they preserve sculptural works which are dated exactly by the decrees accompanying them. These reliefs help in turn in the dating of other works of art (statues, reliefs etc.) or in the identification of certain types of statues. Without being great works of art in themselves, nevertheless they present us with an astounding picture when arranged in chronological order. In this strictly chronological sequence, we see the various styles of sculpture evolving before our eyes, we see the types of gods and goddesses changing in accordance with the artistic trends of the times as they were shaped year by year by the great artists of the classical age. But even more important are perhaps the inscriptions, the decrees engraved below the reliefs. They provide important information about historical events, alliances, wars, honours conferred, cults, etc. From that point of view, these inscriptions are of inestimable value.

1471. Athenian decree of 347/46 B.C., whereby the city of Athens honoured the three sons — Spartakos, Pairisadis and Apollonios — of Leukon, king of Kimmerios Bosporus on the northern shore of the Euxine, for having seen to the supply of Athens with wheat. Over the text of the decree, there is a representation in relief showing the persons honoured, two of them seated and one standing, all dressed in himation. Below the relief, engraved in large lettering is the "summary" of the decree: "For Spartakos, Pairisadis, Apollonios, sons of Leukon".

1467. Marble slab with the engraved text of an alliance treaty concluded between Kerkyra (Corfu) and Athens in 375/4 B.C. Above the text of the treaty, there is a relief showing a man on the left personifying the Athenian people, the goddess Athena in the middle, and a woman personifying Kerkyra, on the right.

1480. Decree of the Athenian parliament and the demos, about a treaty between Neapolis (present day Kavala) and Athens. On the relief, over the decree, Athena, on the left, greets a woman wearing a "polos" on her head; she is the goddess of Neapolis, Parthenos, as we learn from the engraved inscription. It dates from 356 B.C.

Votive reliefs are very important for the history of ancient art, because they are original works reflecting the artistic trends of their time. They are equally important

76. *Attic funerary relief No 3716 known as "far-shining tomb".*

77. *Funerary stele No 870 known as the "goodbye stele" from Athens.*

for the study of ancient religion and worship, because they provide direct evidence of the ideas of the ancients concerning the nature of the gods and the rites of worship. These votive reliefs represent religious practices or scenes of worship, sacrifices, offerings to the gods, common mortals going to the sanctuaries with their gifts — sacrificial animals or bloodless sacrifices — and the gods and goddesses receiving them or watching them, supposedly unseen. Many include inscriptions mentioning the name of the god to whom the offering was dedicated and the name of the sponsor who dedicated it, but almost never the name of the artist who made them. This contrasts with the practice in respect of statues, where the sculptor seldom fails to mention his name. Votive reliefs are an important source of knowledge of the ancient world and they have frequently revealed unknown aspects of ancient worship, they have illustrated myths or have pointed to particularities in the local cult of certain deities.

3917. A relief dedicated to Apollo, Artemis and Leto. It is informative in that the figures of Apollo and Leto are imitations of known originals: the former is an imitation of Apollo Patroos, a work of Euphranor, a celebrated sculptor of the 4th century B.C; Leto is an imitation of an apparently famous statue of the 4th century, some later copies of which have been preserved.

78. One of the loveliest and most famous funerary steles of the 4th century B.C., known as "stele of Ilissos" No 869, the work of an outstanding artist of the school of Skopa.

79. Funerary replica of a temple No 737 from Kerameikos, at the grave of Prokleides Aegialius, his wife Archippe and their son Prokles; this work with the nearly round carved figures represents an advanced stage of the funerary reliefs of the 4th century B.C.

80. *The votive relief of Archinos No 3369 from Amphiareio of Oropos, depicting a medical treatment by Amphiaraos; first half of 4th century B.C.*

3874, 1445, 1448, 2011. The cult of Pan and the Nymphs was widespread in Attica, where many important reliefs and statues dedicated to these deities have been found. As they were usually worshipped in caves, many of these reliefs are shown in a cave setting instead of the usual structural forms consisting of posts and epistyle or, less frequently, a small temple with pediment. The artists thus related the offering to its destined environment. This room contains a large number of votive reliefs, including: No **3874** which shows three Nymphs dancing in front of an altar, from Ekali; No **1445** depicting a similar scene, from Eleusis; No **1448**, with dancing Nymphs and the god Hermes, found in the cave of Mt. Parnes; and No **2011**, again portraying Nymphs and the god Hermes. Never absent from these reliefs is Pan, the goat-footed god of forests, playing the pipe. Animals also seem to be a natural part of these scenes.

The cult of Asklepios, the healing god of Epidaurus, was prevalent in Athens, ever since it was introduced by an Athenian citizen, Telemachos of Acharnae, in the year of the archon Astyphilos 420/19 B.C. This information is due to two interesting inscriptions which give details of the transfer at first of the cult of Asklepios from Piraeus to the "Eleusinion" in Athens. Telemachos was the first to establish a sanctuary of that god in Athens, and that sanctuary was to become important to the Athenians as attested to by the many and valuable offerings that have come down to

81. *Votive relief No* 1332 *of the second half of the 4th century B.C. showing Demeter, Persephone, Asklepios, and the dedicators.*

us. Literary sources inform us also of the decisive role played by the tragic playwright Sophocles in the successful introduction of the cult of Asklepios in Athens. Sophocles was a priest of the healing hero Alo (or Amynos, according to others), whose properties were very similar to those of Asklepios. The Athenians attributed to Sophocles the merit of having "welcomed" Asklepios in Athens and because of this, they erected to him a posthumous monument and attached to him the name of "Dexion". There was a paean to Asklepios by Sophocles, which was sung for many years after the poet's death. Likenesses of the god are often accompanied by his symbols: a serpent coiled around a staff, a pine cone, laurel wreaths, the goat and the dog.

1346. Part of a relief of the early 4th century; it shows Asklepios standing before his altar while he leans on his staff; the two women behind him are his daughters Hygeia and Iaso (Health and Cure).

793. Relief showing the symbol of Asklepios — the serpent.

1338. Relief with posts. On the right, Asklepios seated, upright beside him, the sacred serpent. In the middle, Asklepios' daughter Hygeia is blessing a devotee. Late 5th century B.C.

82. Athenian resolution of 347-46 B.C., honouring the three sons of Leukon, king of Kimmerius Bosporos: Spartakos, Paerisadis and Apollonios.

83. Votive relief No 1402 depicting Asklepios, his two physician-sons Podaleirios and Machaon, his daughters Iaso, Akeso and Panacea, and a family of suppliants; first half of 4th c. B.C.

84. Statue of Asklepios No 258 from Piraeus, the so-called "Asklepios of Munichia", of the second half of the 4th century B.C.

1332. Relief with posts, epistyle and cornice of the 2nd half of the 4th century B.C. Near the left-hand edge, Persephone stands holding two torches while in front of her Demeter is seated on the mystical "kystis" or the fount of goodly dances. Asklepios is standing farther to the right. The right-hand half of the scene is occupied by 6 supplicants in himation. Five of these are the persons dedicating the relief, and their names are engraved inside the olive wreaths seen below the representation. The wreaths indicate that the sponsors, who were Athenian physicians, had been crowned by the city as a token of honour for services rendered. Engraved on the epistyle are the names: *[E... The]odoridis, Epeuches, Mnesitheos,* while beneath the relief and inside the wreaths are the names: *[The]odoridis son of Polykratos, Sostrato[s] son of Epikratos, Epeuche[s] son of Dieuches, Diakritos son of Dieuches, M[n]e[s]i[theos] son of [Mn]esitheos.*

Dieuches, the father of Epeuches and Diakritos, was a famous physician of the early 4th century B.C., belonging to the dogmatic school. He is mentioned by ancient writers and some fragments of his work have been preserved. The father of the fifth sponsor Mnesitheos was an even more renowned physician and the author of several textbooks. Pausanias saw his grave near the Sacred Way and mentions this in his "Periegesis". The sixth figure appearing at the right-hand end of the relief is almost certainly not a physician but either a relative of one of the sponsors or some influential personage otherwise connected with the doctors; based on a few letters still readable over the figure's head, Svoronos has suggested that it represents the géneral Antiphilos. The faces of the figures have been destroyed by hammer blows as a result of the destructive rage of the early Christians in whose eyes every work of ancient art was a witness of heathenism.

temple replica of Aristonautes with the carved figure of the dead man No738, is
t important funerary reliefs of the 4th century B.C.; its importance lies in the
illustrated and in the high artistic quality.

258. Statue of Asklepios from Piraeus, the so-called "Asklepios of Munychia", a work of the later half of the 4th century B.C. The artist was successful in allowing the expression of the god to reveal, as it were, his healing properties. The god was shown standing, dressed in a himation which is visible on the left shoulder and at the back of the body. The left hand rests on the staff, the right hand is at the hip. The eyes were made of a different, coloured, material and must have made the figure look terribly alive.

3369. Another important healing god — revered especially in Attica — was Amphiaraos, one of the seven mythical heroes who marched out against Thebes. His principal sanctuary in Greece was situated at the border between Attica and Boeotia, in the area of ancient Oropos. Its ruins show its great size and the inscriptions found there demonstrate that it was famous all over Greece. An important testimony concerning healing practices at the Amphiareion is the relief No **3369** found in the sanctuary. It dates from the first half of the 4th century and includes posts, an epistyle and a cornice.

Between the molded corner tiles of the cornice, there are two projecting eyes, a mark supposed to avert evil. Standing on the left, Amphiaraos is performing a surgical operation on the shoulder of a standing young man named Archinos. On the right, Archinos appears as a supplicant and in the middle the same is shown sleeping in a bed while a serpent licks his shoulder — apparently the site of his injury. The base bears the following incription: Ἀρχῖνος Ἀμφιαράωι ἀνέθηκεν (Dedicated to Amphiaraos by Archinos).

Room 28, of Aristonautes

738. One of the last funeral sculptures of 4th century Attica is this monument of Aristonautes, son of Archenautes, from Alae, according to the inscription engraved on the epistyle of the pediment crowning the small temple: Aristonautes, son of Archenautes of Alae. The deceased is represented as a young hoplite in battle posture. He wears a chiton and, over this, a corselet, while a chlamys is draped over the left shoulder. He holds the shield in his left hand, while the right hand would be holding the sword. The advanced form of the sculpture — this is no longer the traditional relief of the Attic stele — is one of the criteria classifying this work among the last of its kind in a brilliant series of unique quality and variety. About 310 B.C.

4796. Funeral relief from the great burial precinct of Hierocles at Ramnous. Its adventures cover an entire century. The heads were originally found during unauthorized excavations in 1879 but were eventually purchased by the government. The bodies were attached to the heads much later, and some additional pieces which complete the representation have been found recently. The relief is the work of an Athenian craftsman made around 325 B.C. As suggested by recent research, it portrays Hierocles son of Hiero, head of a great family of Ramnous, one of his five sons, Lyceas, and a relative, Demostrate. It seems likely that the little temple which housed this relief also contained another, showing another son of Hierocles, Iophon.

833. One of the five sons of Hierocles of Ramnous (the one portrayed in relief No 4796) was Hiero, represented here with his wife Lysippe. This relief formed part of a little temple with a pediment. Unencumbered by the presence of the many figures including seated figures, that we have seen in some of the other reliefs, this scene has an air of austerity, enhanced by the tall and slender bodies of the couple, between whom a deep and tender bond is evident. About 325 B.C.

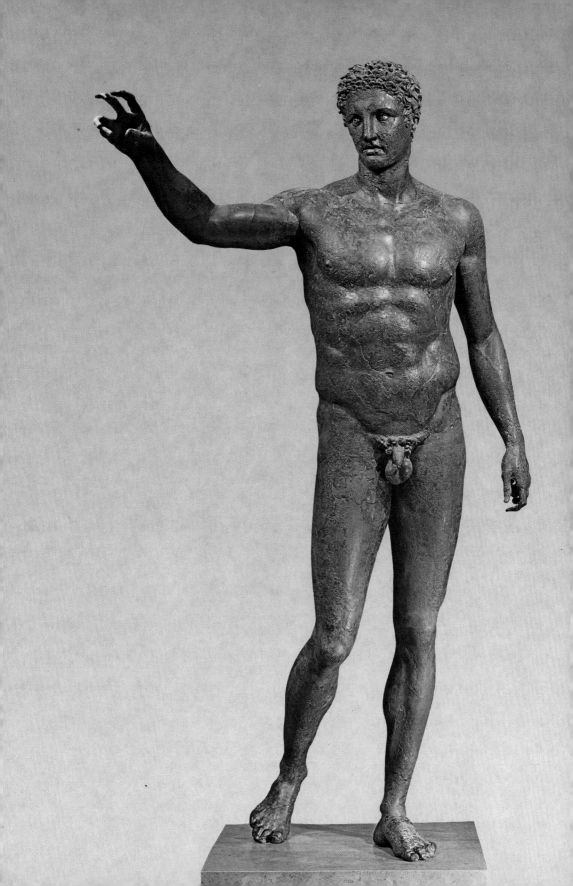

88

87. *The famous bronze statue No 13396 of the "Youth of Antikythera", the work of a Peloponnesian sculptor.* 88. *Marble head No 3602, thought to belong to a statue of Hygieia at the temple of Alea Athena at Tegea.* 89. *Marble head of a goddess No 182 from the theatre of Dionysus; it represents, possibly, Ariadne and is the work of an eminent artist of the second half of the 4th century B.C.* 90. *Marble statue of Themis No 231 from Ramnous, Attica, a work of the sculptor Chaerestratos.*

1283. A post from some funeral temple replica in the cemetery of Ramnous, Attica. Shown is a young slave girl wearing the garment typical of her class. She accompanied her mistress who was probably portrayed in the main scene. About 320 B.C.

4464. Unique in size and artistic audacity, this funeral relief is a precursor of Hellenistic art; it pictures a war horse seen from the side, its back covered with a panther skin, a negro groom with a whip standing in front of it. Traces of painting are visible in the background. The horse and the groom were also coloured. Late 4th - early 3rd century B.C.

Room 29, of the ephebe of Antikythera

13396. One of the most famous archaeological discoveries was that of the ancient shipwreck off Antikythera in 1900. Found among many marble sculptures and other objects of high scientific interest, was this bronze statue of a young man with upraised arm. Its present appearance is the result of long and strenuous efforts by specially trained archaeologists and technicians. When the statue was first found, it was unsuccessfully restored by A. André. Much later, in the first semester of 1953, the statue, which had been taken apart in 1948-49, was reassembled in its present form. There is no certainty as to the identity of the youth of Antikythera: Could it be Perseus holding the head of Medusa? Not very likely. Is it Paris with the apple? Or Herakles? The statue, which is the work of a great Peloponnesian sculptor and dates from about 340 B.C., shows influence of the "Canon" of Polykleitos and of such modern trends as are represented by the great statue-maker Lysippos of Argos.

178-180. The temple of Athena Alea in Tegea, built by the great architect and sculptor Skopa, was ornamented with sculptures in its pediments. The three male heads we see here come from the eastern pediment, which represented the hunt of the Caledonian Boar, a popular theme with the ancients. What ancient information there is does not seem to indicate that Skopa, a native of Paros, was the sculptor responsible for the pediments of the temple, but it is a fact that the sculptures demonstrate all the characteristics of his art "the rectangular shapes, the deep-set eyes, the prominent lower part of the forehead — the marks of powerful and passionate personalities". Skopa, Praxiteles and Euphranor are the three great sculptors who renewed the art in the 4th century B.C. but Skopa is the greatest innovator of the three, the one who introduced elements of "startling originality".

3602. From the ancient traveller Pausanias we know that inside the temple of Athena Alea at Tegea, there were, on either side of the statue of the goddess, statues of Asklepios and Hygeia made from Pentelic marble by the great sculptor Skopa of Paros. This female head is believed, based on solid evidence, to be that of the statue of Hygeia. This goddess, the daughter of Asklepios according to the ancients, is indeed the beautiful expression of the ideal signified by her name Hygeia = Health. About 360 B.C.

1733. A rectangular marble base, which supported an offering awarded as a prize to the winner of an equestrian competition. The same representation is repeated on three sides of the base: a horseman wearing a short chlamys is walking towards a tripod standing on a two-step base. On the fourth, and main, side, there is the following inscription: *φυλαρχοῦντες ἐνίκων ἀνθιππασίαι/Δημαίνετος Δημέο Παιανιεύς / Δημέας Δημαινέτο Παιανιεύς / Δημοσθένης Δημαινέτο Παιανιεύς / Βρύαξις ἐπόησεν.*

The "anthippasia" mentioned in the inscription was an equestrian team game. The Athenian sculptor Vryaxis from Karia of Asia Minor is known mainly for his contribution to the sculptural decoration of the Mausoleum of Alikarnassos. This base serves as a standard of reference for the identification of his work among the sculptures of the Mausoleum. Midddle of 4th century B.C.

Room 30, of Themis

231. There is evidence suggesting that alongside Nemesis, another goddess was worshipped in the great Attic sanctuary of Ramnous - Themis, goddess of Justice. This statue of Themis, dedicated by Megakles, son of Megakles of Ramnous and made by the sculptor Chaerestratos, also of Ramnous, was found in the smaller temple of the sanctuary. Investigators have suggested, though without any certainty, that the goddess held a bronze scales in one hand and a flask for libations in the other. Carefully and competently made, the statue is nevertheless a rather cold adaptation of earlier art concepts. First half of 3rd century B.C.

1734-1737, 2171-2175. In the arcadic town of Lykosoura, there was a sanctuary of the chthonian goddess Despina (Persephone) whose cult under that name was limited to the confines of Arcadia. Around the 4th century temple of the goddess, there were a number of altars and an arcade. Standing on a great pedestal at the far end of the nave of the temple was a group of larger-than-life statues showing Demeter and Despina seated on thrones between Artemis and the Titan Anytos who were standing. The statues were made by the Messenian sculptor Damophon (other works of the same sculptor existed in Messene, Megalopolis and elsewhere). The greatest part of the Lykosoura group has been preserved and can be seen in the

91

91. *Marble head from a statue of the great Athenian orator and politician Demosthenes, a copy of the 2nd century B.C.*

local museum. Displayed here are the heads of Demeter (1734), Artemis (1735) and Anytos (1736) (Despina's head has not been preserved); also a large fragment of the folds of the himation of Despina (1737) and Tritons and Tritonesses from the throne of the gods (2171-2172, 2174-2175). These works too bear evidence of imitation of older works or trends. 2nd century B.C.

327. A well-known work of the Athenian sculptor Polyeuctos was the bronze statue of the great Athenian orator Demosthenes, made around 280 B.C., i.e. some 40 years after the death of Demosthenes in 322 B.C. Several copies of that statue have been preserved, including some 15 heads, of which this is one, dating from the 2nd century A.D. The statue showed the orator wringing his hands, "to suggest anguish and grief. It was clearly the sculptor's intention to represent Demosthenes not as a great orator and literary writer, but as a politician who all his life struggled in vain to defend an ideal and on whose face bitterness and frustration had left deep scars" (Ch. Tsountas). On the base of this statue, the Athenians later engraved the famous epigram. If your body, Demosthenes, were as strong as your mind, Mars from Macedonia would never conquer Greece.

215-217. These three marble slabs together with one or more others, formed the outer surface of the base of the statues of Apollo and Leto made, according to the traveller Pausanias, by Praxiteles for the temple of Leto and her children in Mantineia, where the slabs were found by the French School of Archaeology in 1887. One of the slabs shows the musical contest between Apollo and Marsyas. Wearing a floor-length chiton and himation, Apollo, on the left, is sitting on a rock with his guitar; on the right, the satyr Marsyas, naked, is playing his double flute with all his force; standing in the middle, the Scythian slave is holding the knife with which he is going to skin Marsyas. Each of the other two slabs pictures three Muses in different postures, "charming examples of clothed female figures of the 4th century". It is generally accepted that the reliefs on the slabs were not made by Praxiteles but by some assistant in his workshop, according to the great artist's instructions. The figures on the slabs clearly reflect the spirit of his art. About 320 B.C.

Room 31, of the Poseidon of Melos

6439. Bronze head from the statue of the pugilist Satyros, son of Lysianax from Eleia who, according to the traveller Pausanias, had won five times at Nemea, two at Delphi and two at Olympia. It is almost certain that the head belongs to the statue of the athlete made by the Athenian sculptor Silanion. The artist has rendered very realistically the "unlikeable" type of the professional prize fighter with his crooked ears, the bashed-in nose, his energy and brute force. But he has also succeeded in lending spirituality to his very unspiritual subject.

13400. The ancient shipwreck from which came the famous "ephebe of Antikythera" also produced the bronze head known as the "philosopher of Antikythera". It belonged to the statue of an unknown man dressed in a himation, of the later half of the 3rd century B.C. Also preserved from that statue are the right arm, the left hand, the right foot and part of the left foot. The expression and the deliberate ugliness of the head, the untidy hair, the beard, the thick mustache, and the realistic rendering of the features, immediately created the impression that this was a likeness of a cynic philosopher and it was in fact suggested that it might be Bion of Borysthena. He was a freed bondsman, deeply influenced by the Athenian environment where he lived, and who spent some time in the Court of the Macedonian king Antigonos Gonatas. His *"diatribes* crusaded against passions and prejudices" (A. Lesky) and, as we know from Horatio, were very influential in antiquity. Bion's name was indeed used as an attribute to characterize particularly caustic satire. Regardless of whether the head portrays Bion or some other person, the fact remains that the unknown sculptor has rendered his model with unique force and spiritual depth - which proves him to be an uncommonly gifted artist.

232. This statue comes from the sanctuary of Nemesis at Ramnous, Attica, and represents Aristonoe, a priestess of the goddess. It was found together with its base which is engraved with an inscription. According to the inscription, the statue was dedicated to Nemesis and Themis by Aristonoe's son Hierokles. Based on internal evidence, it is dated to the second half of the 3rd century B.C.

235. Larger-than-life statue of the god Poseidon, from Melos. The statue is made of two pieces, joined at about the level of the waist. The god is shown standing, leaning on his right leg. There was a trident in his raised right hand, while the left hand rests on the hip. Near his right foot there is a dolphin with upright tail. The statue has external magnificence but lacks the vital inner force we find in earlier works. It has been remarked that "the artist has given all his attention to the external form, with the intention of producing a strong effect on the spectator's senses". About 130 B.C.

14612. In the previous rooms, we saw two excellent bronze portraits — one of the pugilist Satyros, and one of a - supposedly - cynical philosopher. This head from Delos, part of a bronze statue of an unknown man honoured there, is of later date — early 1st century B.C. The head looks unusually alive, an effect enhanced by the inlaid eyes of a different material, as in the case of the philosopher of Antikythera. The artist's intention in shaping the face was clearly not to produce beauty but to express inner life.

3335. This group of Aphrodite and Pan, from Delos, dating from around 100 B.C. reflects not only the prevailing concept of art in its time, but also the concept of divinity prevailing among artists. Likenesses of the goddess had been produced

92. Bronze head No 6439 from the statue of the pugilist and Olympic winner Satyros, form Olympia. 93. Bronze head No 13400 from the shipwreck of Antikythera, probably the head of a philosopher.

earlier by great creators, such as Pheidias, Alkamenes, Kalamis and Praxiteles. Their works were expressions of respect for the Olympian goddess. Here the artist has chosen to show her in an amusing scene. The goat-footed Pan is half embracing her while she threatens to hit him with her sandal. The winged Eros assists his mistress by pushing Pan away. The expressions on all three faces show that the episode is an insignificant occurrence in their everyday lives. The also preserved engraved base informs us that the group was dedicated by a Syrian merchant to the gods of his country.

This is a far way off from the reverential votive reliefs of the 5th and 4th century. This sculpture already presages the death of the ancient religion, the death of Pan himself though it would be another two centuries before his death was announced, as Plutarch tells the story, by an Egyptian ship's pilot named Thamous who, obeying a mysterious voice he had heard near Paxoi, called out as he was sailing by Palodes: Πᾶν ὁ μέγας τέθνηκε (The great Pan is dead).

3377. The ancient traveller Pausanias tells about the existence of a sanctuary of Zeus at Aegira in Achaia, and describes a statue of the god in that sanctuary: it showed Zeus seated, and was made from Pentelic marble by the Athenian sculptor Eukleides. This partly preserved head of Zeus is believed to be the head of that statue. The work is impressive by its sheer size; it expresses a creative classicism drawing on the great masters of the past, on the technique of earlier works and their majestic style. To judge by this fragment of the head, Eukleides' Zeus was three times larger than life-size. 2nd century B.C.

94. Oversize marble statue of Poseidon No 235 from Melos; the right hand probably held a trident; a dolphin at the right thigh served as support for the statue.

95. Statue of Aristonoe No 232, a priestess of Nemesis at Ramnous, dedicated by her son Hierokles to the sanctuary of the goddess. According to the inscription at the pedestal of the statue, the offering was dedicated not only to the goddess Nemesis but also to Themis, another deity worshipped at the temple.

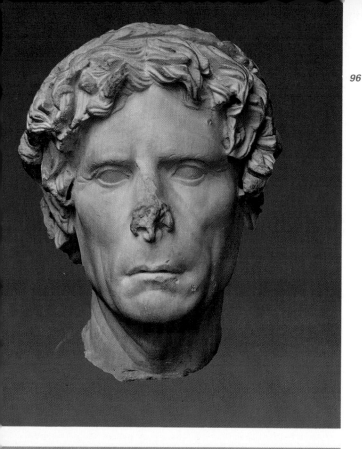

96. Excellent head (portrait) No 351 from the statue of a priest, the work of an Attic workshop of the 1st century B.C.

97. Bronze head portrait No 14612 from Delos; of exquisite execution, with inlaid eyes, it expresses passion and inner life.

98. Marble group No 3335, representing Aphrodite, Pan and Eros; showing technical knowledge and daring, this group was dedicated by a Syrian merchant to the gods of his homeland.

99. Gold necklaces from the Stathatos collection dating from the 4th and 3rd centuries B.C. and offering a wide variety of decorative elements: Silenus heads (No 344), spear-shaped leaves suspended from rosettes (No 340), and rosettes with suspended acorns and bullheads (No 306).

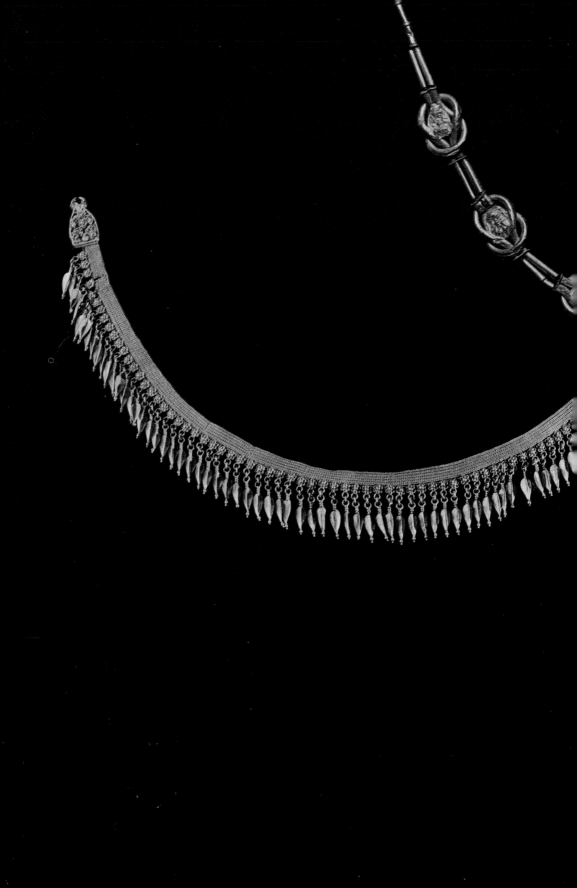

Room 32, collection of Eleni Stathatou

Jewel-making is one of the oldest arts. Along with his struggle for survival, man has always been keen on his embellishment. In the rooms of prehistoric collections, we saw jewellery from every cultural period in the prehistory of Greece. The Mycenaeans were masters in the making of jewellery and their creations are justly admired. The exhibits in this room were not found at systematic excavations and there is no unity between them. They are the collection donated to the Greek state by Mrs. Eleni Stathatou, a collection that took many years and a great deal of effort to achieve. The most valuable pieces are the jewels, some of which are of unique artistry or originality. The collection represents Greek gold-smithery and jewel-making from antiquity down to the Byzantine period.

100. *Gold temple replica No 379 with relief likeness of Dionysus, satyr and panther, of the late 3rd century B.C.* **101.** *Gold Hellenistic diadem No 339 from Thessaly.* **102.** *Gold bracelet No 591, possibly of the Roman period, adorned with spirals of a scaly serpent.*

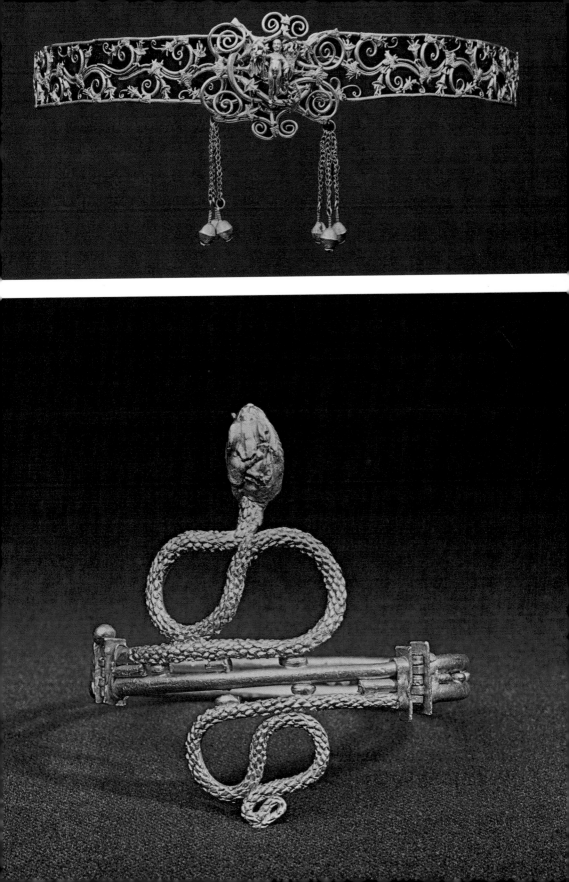

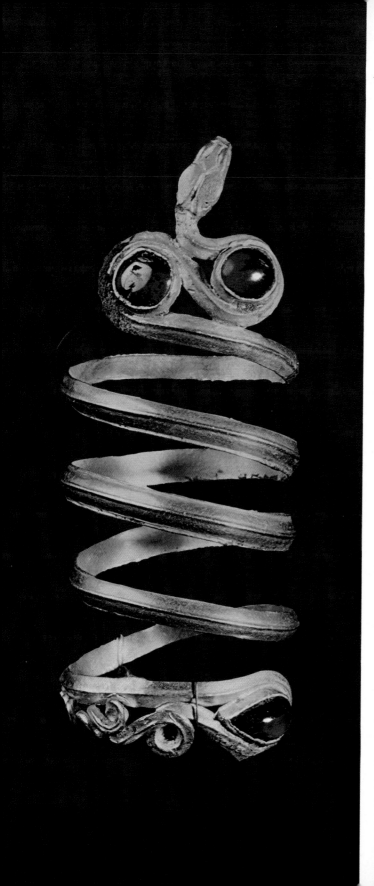

103. *Gold, snake-shaped Hellenistic ring No 354 with three Chalcedonians.*

104. *Gold hairpin No 347 with likeness of Aphrodite and Eros, possibly of the Roman period.*

105. *Gold Byzantine bracelet with Chalcedonian, of the 5th or 6th century A.D.*

106. *Gold Byzantine jewellery for the head No 493 and No 740.*

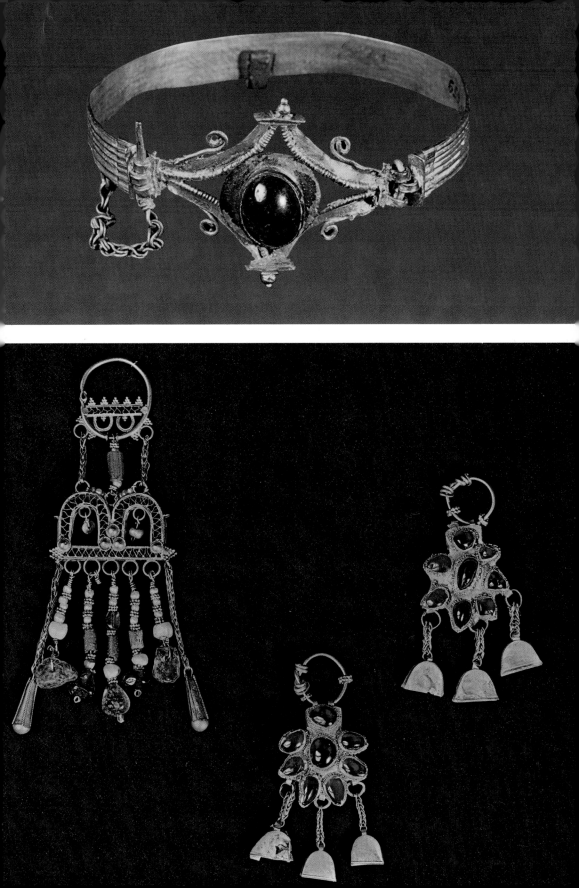

107. Gold pendant No 310 with two sphinxes facing each other, of the 7th century B.C., the work of a workshop of Argos.

108. Two almost identical gold snake-shaped bracelets No 346 A-B, decorated with precious stones.

109. Two gold hanging earrings No 309 with representation of Potnia Theron (tamer of wild beasts) of the 7th century B.C.

110. Gold Byzantine earrings No 510.

THE COLLECTION OF BRONZES

Room 36, of Dodone (Carapanos collection)

The oracle of Zeus in Dodone. At a distance of 22 km from Yannina lies Dodone with the ruins of a sanctuary of Zeus Naios, which was believed by the ancient Greeks to be the earliest Greek oracle. The first major investigation of the great sanctuary was conducted by the Epirus Greek Const. Carapanos, in 1875, when Epirus was still under Turkish rule. Carapanos donated his important finds to the Greek state, and this is the collection kept in this room. Excavations at Dodone were resumed by D. Evangelidis and S. Dakaris after the liberation of Epirus.

The cult of Zeus at Dodone was somewhat different from that in the sanctuaries of the god in the rest of Greece. According to the poet Hesiod, Dodone was the dwelling-place on earth of the king of gods and men; he lived, specifically, in the sacred oak. His priests were the Selloi, a clan of hereditary diviners. The Selloi slept on the ground and they never washed their feet - religious customs whose origin goes back to prehistoric times. While Hera was the wife of Zeus everywhere else, his wife in Dodone was Dione.

Originally, the oracles were given by the rustle of the leaves of Zeus' oak or by the cry or the flight of the pigeons living in the sacred tree. But from the 6th century B.C. onwards, the applicant for an oracle had to write his question on a piece of lead plate. The answer was given orally or even in writing. Many such lead plates have been preserved. Several were found during the excavations of Carapanos and will be seen in the show-cases 1 and 2.

Showcase 1-2: Dodone. Metal plates with engraved parts of vases, handle and handle appendages, decrees engraved on metal.

Base No 540. Veiled female statuette holding a pigeon, from Pindos. About 460 B.C.

On the wall, No 16857. Tripods were not only useful utensils, but in their better bronze forms, they were frequently used as offerings to gods or as prizes at competitions, ever since the time of Homer. This is the leg of a large tripod ornamented with geometric decorative designs. Perhaps from Dodone, 8th century B.C.

Show-case 3: Figurines, vase handles, metal plates with imprinted representations. No **31,** statuette of Zeus holding and about to hurl the thunderbolt; No **166,** cheekpiece (Paragnathis) of helmet with imprinted scene showing two naked warriors with excellent plasticity and movement. Early 4th century B.C.

Base No 16546. Statuette of Zeus holding and about to hurl the thunderbolt, contiguous with brick base, from Dodone.

Base, No 27+16547. Rider and horse, from Dodone. The rider comes from the excavations of Carapanos, in 1875, while the horse was found in 1956. Although shown here as a group, the horse actually belonging to the rider - one of the same size as this - is in the Louvre. The horse shown here was match to another rider, not found as yet. The certain existence of the two groups has led to the assumption that they represented the two brothers of Helen, the Dioscuri. Middle of 6th century B.C.

112

111. *Bronze statuette of a flute player No 25, of the 6th century B.C.*

112. *Rider on horseback No 27+16547 from Dodone, of the 6th cent. B.C.*

113. *Statuette of Zeus No 16546 of the 5th century B.C. from Dodone.*

113

Show-case 4: Bronzes from various parts of Greece, mainly vases, human and animal figurines, utensil handles. Of interest is the frying-pan No **557** with a kouros-shaped handle. Late 6th century B.C.

Base No 25. Statuette of a flute-player of the late 6th century B.C. in a long chiton - a theme as frequent in small sculpture as in vase-painting. Hanging on his left arm is the sheath for the flutes. He is playing the flutes, while his face is constricted by the halter.

Show-case 7: Bronzes from Dodone: fragments of tripods with engraved geometric designs, vase handles and added-on decorations, lion feet from tripods. No **24,** statuette of a runner used as decoration of bronze vase, probably produced by a workshop of Laconia in the second half of the 6th century B.C.; No **36,** statuette of a young horseman, used as vase decoration, also coming from Laconia.

Show-case 8: Bronzes from Dodone: jewels, weapons, vase handle. No **803,** small bronze column with pediment ornamented with acroteriums, an offering to Zeus by Agathon, son of Echephylos of Zante, and his family who had been consuls of the Molossans of Epirus for thirty generations, starting with Cassandra of Troy:

"Θεός: τύχα Ζεῦ Δωδώνης μεδέων, / τῆσε σοι δῶρον πέμπτω παρ' ἐμοῦ, 'Αγάθων 'Εχεφύλου καί γενεά, πρόξενο: / Μολοσσῶν καὶ συμμάχων ἐν τριάκοντα γενεαῖς ἐκ Τρωίας Κασσάνδρας, / γενεᾶ Ζακύνθιοι".

The male organ shown in relief symbolizes the productive power of nature and, specifically, that of the genealogy of Agathon: No **19,** little dancing Maenad, an accessory of a bronze crater, her posture showing her exhaustion from her orgiastic dance; No **18,** small statuette of a comic actor. 4th c. B.C.

Show-case 8A: Bronzes from various parts of Greece, vases, vase handles and statuettes. No **16727,** bronze statuette of a general of the 4th century B.C., possibly from Dodone, wearing a short chiton, helmet and corselet, barefoot, holding a (now missing) spear in his left hand and, in his right hand, the liver of an animal, possibly sacrificed before the battle for divination purposes.

No 968. Marble stele with "Ioutrophoros" in relief. Along the left-hand edge, there is the epigram: "Here lies a man from the holy earth of Lemnos, who loved (his) sheep. His name was Nikomachos". High up on the broad part of the "Ioutrophoros", there is the inscription: Nikomachos of Piraeus.

Nos 784-794. Replica of Roman chariot; placed on it are the bronze accessories and decorations of the original, a chariot from Nikomedia in Asia Minor.

Room 37, bronzes from Olympia and other sites

(*Room 37. Temporarily closed from Olympia bronzes to no 7913 pp. 130-142.*)

Olympia bronzes: The two greatest and most important sanctuaries in ancient Greece were Olympia and Delphi. The former, where Apollo was worshipped, soon acquired great political and religious power and became "the arbitrator and the guardian of right faith and thinking". In the sanctuary of Olympia, which lies in a valley of the river Alpheios and is surrounded by low hills, Zeus was worshipped, the king of gods and men. In the earliest years, prior to the archaic period, the sanctuary had a tradition of divination. As such, it was later overshadowed by Dodone, while athletic games became increasingly important to Olympia, finally developing into the main activity of the sanctuary. The Olympic Games were held every four years in honour of Zeus.

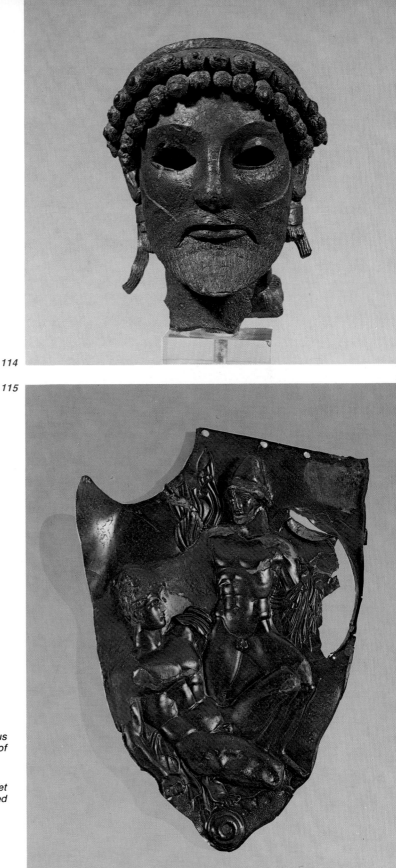

114

115

114. Bronze head of Zeus from Olympia No 6440 of the 5th century B.C.

115. Side piece of helmet No 166 showing two naked warriors.

116

116. *Statuette of a woman holding a pigeon No 540.* **117.** Geometric statuette depicting a hoplite No 12831.

Participants came from every part of Greece, and some of the victors, like Hiero of Syracuse, Thero from Akragas, Diagoras of Rhodes, were glorified by Pindar. According to that poet, the Olympic Games were instituted by Herakles, though local tradition attributed the initiation of the Games to Pelops, after his victory over Oenomaos.

The offerings and buildings discovered at the excavation of Olympia are invaluable for the study of ancient Greek art. The sculptures of the pediments and the metopes of the temple of Zeus, Hermes of Praxiteles, the head of Hera, the Nike of Paeonion, the bronze head of a satyr (room **31** No **6439**) give the measure of Olympia's importance for us today. Particularly useful for the study of ancient bronze art are the bronze offerings to Zeus found by the thousands during the excavations: they include small animals, griffins, weapons, cauldrons, tripods, ornamental objects, plates with representations. Many of those found at the earlier excavations of Olympia in the last century are in this room. More recent finds are kept in the museum of Olympia.

ΘΕΟΣ ΤΥΧΑ

8

119

118. *Bronze stele from Dodone inscribed with epigram No 803.* **119.** *Statuette depicting a general of the 4th c. B.C. No* 16727.

Show-case 9: Bronzes from Boeotia and other sites, of the geometric and archaic periods, jewels (mainly broaches), human and animal statuettes. Worthy of note is the bronze belt No **8602** of the 5th century B.C., from Plataea, with affixed ox-heads.

Base No 7582. Bronze head of griffin used as cauldron decoration.

Base No 6443. Metal plate showing kneeling Herakles with bow, from Olympia.

Base No 6442. Bronze column with posts and pediment. On the pediment bunch of grapes in relief between two double axes, symbols of Tenedos. Engraved on the cap is a resolution of the Elians honouring "Demokrates, son of Agetor, of Tenedos" in the 3rd century B.C. for his victory in the wrestling competition at the Olympic Games. As we learn from the traveller Pausanias, there was at Olympia a statue of Demokrates, made by the sculptor Dionysokles of Miletus. One of his wrestling feats at Olympia is told by Aelianos, a writer of the 2nd-3rd century A.D.

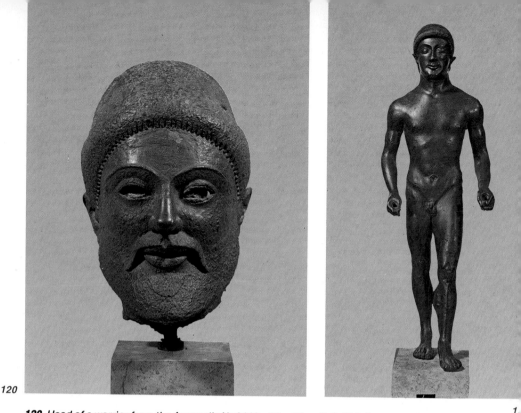

120. Head of a warrior from the Acropolis No 6446 of the 5th c. B.C. 121. Statuette of an athlete from the Acropolis No 6445, late 6th c. B.C.

Base No 16512. Bronze fountain in the form of a lion head from the Heraeon of Samos. A frog sitting on the lion head watched the flowing water. 7th century B.C.

Base No 6163. From Olympia. Statuette of Zeus with long himation and stretched out arms, of the late 6th century B.C., of Peloponnesian origin.

Show-case 12: Olympia. Bronze figurines of humans and animals, vase handles etc., of the geometric and archaic periods, found during the excavation of the temple of Zeus the last century.

Base No 6440. Olympia. An excellent head of Zeus, of the austere style. Early 5th century B.C.

Base No 6444. Olympia. Bronze plate, possibly an ornament of a wooden box. Molded in four bands from the bottom upwards are shown: Winged Artemis as mistress of hunting, holding a lion by its hindlegs in each hand, Herakles aiming an arrow at a Centaur, two griffins facing each other and, in the uppermost band, three eagles.

Show-case 10: Olympia. Human and animal statuettes found at earlier excavations of Olympia. No **7941,** flask with molded decoration; No **6133,** miniscule intact tripod, with birds on the handles of the cauldron supported by it; No **7483,** circular handle of cauldron, with a small decorative horse.

Show-case 11: Olympia. Bronze finds from last century's excavations, including animals and griffins, mainly of the archaic period. No **6122-6123,** affixed decorations incl. human head, bird feathers and tail — a theme imported from the east. No **6120, 6162,** heads of griffins used to decorate small cauldrons; No **6139,** matrix of small Daedalic head for add-on decoration.

Bases No 6159, 6160. Olympia. Heads of griffins used to decorate bronze cauldrons.

Show-case 12, Olympia. Human and animal statuettes of the geometric and archaic periods, broaches; No **6236,** seven women, forming a circle as they embrace, performing a religious dance; No **6164,** bronze plate with the historical inscription-epigram engraved on it:

Ἑλλήνων ἦρχον τότ' Ὀλυμπίαι, ἡνίκα μοι Ζεύς | δῶκεν νικῆσαι πρῶτον
Ὀλυμπιάδα |
ἵπποις ἀθλοφόροις, τὸ δὲ δεύτερον αὗτις ἐφεξῆς | ἵπποις,
υἱὸς δ' ἦν Τρωΐλος Ἀλκινόου

A statue of this Troilos, son of Alkinoos, the winner mentioned in the epigram, was seen by Pausanias at Olympia. Troilos was a member of the jury *(hellanodikes)* at the time of his first victory in 372 B.C. (102nd Olympiad). In the following Olympics in 368 B.C. (103rd Olympiad) he won again. After his first victory, according to Pausanias, the Elians passed a law forbidding members of the jury to compete in the chariot races. The statue of Troilos at Olympia was a work of the great sculptor Lysippos; No **6135,** metal plate showing the Minotaur being killed by Theseus.

Show-case 13: Bronzes from Phthiotis and Thessaly, mainly jewels, such as small broaches or little birds of the late geometric period.

Base No 12831. Geometric bronze statuette of a naked hoplite with helmet, figure-of-eight shield thrown over his back, and broad belt.

Show-case 14: Bronzes from various sites: helmets, human and animal statuettes. No **16514,** belt from Kerastari of Arcadia, first half of the 7th century B.C. showing two warriors with figure-of-eight shields, and chariots on their right and left; No **7842,** handle of cauldron with little horse.

Show-case 15: Bronzes from the Peloponnese: No **13056,** miniature kouros, the head covered with a "pole" made of leaves or feathers in a ray-like arrangement. In front, the hair falls in long curls reaching down to the chest; the left hand encircles a cock, the right held perhaps a spear; No **13060,** statuette representing a heavily clothed shepherd; No **13054,** fox hanging by its hindlegs; No **14765,** statuette of naked, bearded warrior with helmet; Nos **13057, 13059, 13061, 13062,** small figurines from Berekla of Olympia.

Show-case 16: Offerings from Mt. Ptoon and Kavirion of Boeotia, animal statuettes and figurines; No **7382,** kouros from Ptoon, made by an Argive artist; No **7412,** discus-thrower; No **7388,** kore from Ptoon; No **7384,** two fragments of the mouth of a cauldron with affixed figure of woman with feathers and tail of a bird.

Bronzes from the Acropolis: The excavation of the Acropolis produced a series of bronze works of art, mainly of small size, offerings to Athena who was worshipped there. These offerings present a wide variety: statuettes, cauldrons, weapons, utensils, vases, such as flasks; many of these were offered by humble craftsmen or tradesmen and represented part of their first earnings.

The sanctuary of the goddess Athena on the Acropolis did not enjoy the prestige of Delphi or Olympia, but it was the national sanctuary of the Athenians and the quality of offerings to the goddess corresponded to the high level of Attic art.

Base No 6446. Head of warrior from the Acropolis. The now missing helmet and the eyes were added. Its form closely resembles the figures in the pediments of the temple of Aphaea in Aegina, which suggests that it is the work of an artist from Aegina. Believed to have been dedicated to Athena by a general or by a winner of the hoplite race. 490-480 B.C.

Base No 15137. Bronze hydria from Eretria. The horizontal handles are decorated with anthemions, the vertical one with rams and a Daedalic female head in the lower part, and with lions in the upper part. The leaden lid has also been preserved.

Base No 14984. Statuette of Zeus hurling the thunderbolt, from Ambrakia; the god is shown naked and bearded; he holds the thunderbolt in one hand, while an eagle rests on the back of his outstretched left hand. About 490 B.C.

Base No 16768. Statuette of Athena Promachos (fighting Athena) from the sanctuary of the goddess in Phocis. First half of the 5th century B.C.

Base No 6445. Statuette of naked athlete, from the Acropolis. Left foot forward, the hands probably held dumb-bells. Attic work with Ionic influence. About 500 B.C.

Show-case 18: From the Acropolis. Animals (cocks), sphinxes, griffin heads. Nos **6475, 6476, 6478, 6479, 6480:** winged Victories, as utensil accessories; shown in flight with bent knees, a conventional posture intended to suggest rapid flying. Graceful small works, adding variety to a recurring theme.

122. Handle of a bronze vessel showing four figures No 6511.

123. Statuette of Athena No 6447 shown in a warlike stance (Promachos).

124. Head of a youth of the 5th century B.C. No 6590 from Acropolis.

Show-case 21: From the Acropolis. Human statuettes and fragments of similar larger works (legs, arms), animals.

Show-case 19: From the Acropolis. Spear points, vase handles, statuettes, figures from circular cauldron handles, small horses, affixed moldings in the form of female heads with bodies and feathers of birds. No **6951,** small bronze base of a not preserved statuette, with the inscription: *Pheidiades dedicated (the offering) to Athena''.* 6th century B.C. **No 6509, 6510,** two excellent gorgonions with serpents coming out of them; No **6506,** little owl, symbol of the goddess Athena; No **6941,** small base of a lost offering with the inscription: *Dedicated to Athena by Aeschines and Charias, from their first earnings.* 6th century B.C.

Show-case 23: From the Acropolis. Figurines, which were accessories of utensils dedicated by Athenians. No **6511,** handle of a vase ornamented with four charming figures: Herakles, Hermes (the lower part with the winged sandals is preserved), and two others; No **7038,** bronze replica of ship with the inscription: *"Sanctuary of Athena"*; No **6837,** small bronze shield decorated with a gorgonion in the middle, dedicated to Athena by Phrygia, owner of a bakery as suggested by the inscription: *Φρυγία: ἀνέθεκέ μ[ε τ] ἀθ[ε]ναίαι, he ἀρτοπōλ[ις].* Dedicated to Athena by Phrygia, the bread-seller).

Show-case on the wall. No **16128-16143:** Arrow and spear points, made of iron or bronze, together with other objects found in the area of the battle of Thermopylae.

Base No 6447. Statuette of Athena Promachos. The goddess is shown in a warlike posture. She is wearing a himation falling in harmonious folds and visible beneath that is a double chiton. It is believed that the *aegis* on the chest was covered with a sheet of gold. The helmet is decorated with a tall plume resting on the head and neck of a swan. Engraved on the base is the inscription "Μελησό ἀνέθεκεν δεκάτεν τ᾽ Ἀθεναίαι" (Meleso dedicated from one-tenth of her earnings to Athena). Early 5th century B.C.

Show-case 20: Bronzes from various sites, small offerings from the Amyclaeon of Sparta, human and animal statuettes; mirrors with handles in the form of girls: the mirror, that most necessary adjunct to the care of a woman's beauty, appears in a wide variety of fine works of art covering the whole span from the archaic to the classical period. The most interesting examples in this show-case are: No **7703**, perhaps from Aegina, dating from about 560 B.C. The girl shown stands on a tortoise; interposed between her head and the disc are the helices of a capital held in the figure's hand; No **11691**, mirror from Corinth, preserved in excellent condition. The kore serving as a support is dressed in a himation and Ionic chiton; the left hand grasps the garment, the outstretched right hand holds a bird; resting on the girl's shoulders are two sphinxes, each using one front paw to hold the support of the mirror; the hair falls in symmetric tresses; about 520 B.C. Other noteworthy mirrors are Nos **7465, 15226, 16214;** they belong to the same type as the one mentioned above.

Show-case 24: Bronzes from the Peloponnese: mainly human and animal figurines, weapons: No **14921** from Tegea, likeness of Persephone on plate; details are indicated by engraved lines; the goddess is dressed in chiton and himation and holds a flask and a torch. No **13220**, bronze jamb; No **14789**, statuette of Spartan warrior with Corinthian helmet, chiton and corselet. No **13209**, figurine of Zeus, shown seated, in Ionic chiton and himation, holding the thunderbolt in his left hand. The god's throne has not been preserved. Late 6th century B.C. No **14922**, Persephone sitting on throne; middle of 5th century B.C.

Base No 6590. From the Acropolis: small head of youth, about 480 B.C., hair gathered in a bun at the back.

Base No 15124. From the area of Lepanto (Naupaktos). Bronze plate with inscriptions on both sides. Late 6th century B.C.

Show-case 26: In the show-case No 20 of the previous room, we saw archaic mirrors with handles in the shape of a young girl.

In this room, we can see some similar types of mirrors, though the differences between the two periods are striking. Reflected in miniature in this series is the great Peloponnesian sculpture and bronze-casting art of the 5th century B.C. represented by a startling variety of one of its characteristic forms, the veiled female figure. Mirror No **7576** is a fine example of the new mirror forms. Dressed in an Ionic-Laconic veil, the girl figure stands on a three-legged support; the right hand is raised, the other is concealed in the folds of the veil. Two small Eros figures hover over her head; the lovely anthemion interposed between the girl and the disc rests on the kore's head.

Innovation - oriented artists in the 5th century created a new type — the folding mirror, *the ptyktos*, i.e. a mirror where the disc was covered when not in use; in the more sophisticated specimens, the cover itself was set with moulded ornaments. Mirror No **7417** from Eretria dates from 420 B.C. approximately, and though not found in Attica, is considered to be an Attic work. It is the earliest known example of the new type. It is decorated on both sides, one side picturing Aphrodite on a swan, the other showing Selene (the Moon) emerging from the sea on horseback; a dolphin is in front of the horse's hooves. Mirror No **16114** from Demetrias of Thessaly dates from the early 3rd century B.C. and is decorated with a female head, while No **16111** also from Demetrias but in silver, shows Selene and Endymion (early 3rd century). Hovering over the frightened-looking young man is a small Eros, while a dog is exiting to the left. According to a myth, Selene fell in love with Endymion, a young and good-looking shepherd. To stop him from growing old, Selene asked Zeus to let him sleep forever, and Zeus granted her wish. Mirror No **7416** from Eretria (abt. 330 B.C.) illustrates another myth: the abduction of Oreythia, daughter of the king of Athens Erechtheus by Boreas, the god of the north wind. Other themes represented among the mirrors in this room include: No **7670,** Aphrodite and Eros on one side, Dionysos and Ariadne on the other (abt. 410 B.C.); No **16115** from Athens, Nike sacrificing a bull (abt. 340 B.C.); No **1448** from Thebes, a satyr and a maenad; No **7672** from Corinth, Aphrodite on horseback; No **7424** from Corinth, head of a woman.

125. Bronze figurine of a flute-player no 16513 *from the Heraeon of Samos.*

126. Bronze head of a griffin no 15205 *used to decorate a bonze cauldron, from Tsotyli, Macedonia.*

127 b.

127 a,b. The famous bronze statue of the "Youth of Marathon" No 15118, possibly a work of Praxiteles.

Base No 7913. Bronze hydria (*kalpis*) from Eretria but made in Attica (4th century B.C.). Pictured below the vertical handle is a separately cast scene of a drunken Dionysos being supported by an equally drunken Satyr.

Ancient bronze sculpture. In gallery 15 we saw the most wonderful bronze statue to have survived from antiquity, the so-called Poseidon, salvaged from the depths of the sea off Cape Artemision in Euboia. As it is not mentioned in any ancient text, it would seem that even more beatiful sculptures existed in ancient Greece. Alongside the great works, however, minor *objets d'art,* domestic utensils, cult vessels and votive offerings had been fashioned since Geometric times and even earlier. Not all of these can be qualified as works of art, indeed in many cases they are found in such large numbers that they were evidently "mass-produced" by ancient standards. However, many are true works of art, whether they be appendages for cauldrons, such as griffins, or statuettes of humans or animals which the devout offered to a deity. The poor pilgrim to a sanctuary dedicated, according to his possibilities, sculpted works which reflected great art.

No 15118. Caught in the nets of fishermen in the Gulf of Marathon in June 1925, this exquisite bronze statue, was named the "Ephebe of Marathon". The statue pictures the god Hermes, and the first archaeologist, K. Romeos, who studied it, supposed that he was examining a turtle. The left arm was subsequently repaired (Buschor) and it has been suggested that in later years, the statue was used as a lamp stand at the villa of Herodes Atticus in Marathon. The sculptor is unknown but he certainly was one of the great artists of the 4th century, and even Praxiteles himself has been suggested.

128. Bronze figurine of a hoplite no 15182 found in Pharsala, Thessaly.

129. Bronze mirror No 7576 with the likeness of a young woman on the handle.

Exhibited in the several cases around the outstanding statue of the Ephebe of Marathon are many important works of ancient Greek bronze sculpting. The case which explains, with models, the way in which bronze statues were cast is particularly illuminating in helping us to understand how these works were made. Standing on a separate base is the flautist no. **16513**, clad in a long sleeved chiton, his cheeks pressed by the leather straps (phorbeia) holding the flute. This work, dated 550-525 B.C., comes from the large sanctuary of Hera on Samos.

Of the pieces in the cases, mention should be made of the bronze statuette of a hoplite, no. **15182**, from Pharsala in Thessaly. Its style and general modelling suggest it was produced in a local workshop in the second half of the sixth century B.C.

The small griffin head no. **15205**, found at Tsotyli in Macedonia, was an ornament for a bronze cauldron and dates from the seventh century B.C. Very similar is the griffin head no. **16417**, from the sanctuary of Thaulios Zeus at Pherres in Thessaly, explored by Apostolos Arvanitopoulos. The little horses nos **18736** and **18737** were also recovered from this site, as well as jewellery, fibulae, pins, birds and even daggers. The small relief warrior no. **7550**, in the same case, merits attention too. Dated to the early fifth century B.C., it decorated a krater, a large open bronze vase, and its probable provenance is Edessa in Macedonia.

Displayed in separate case are bronze finds from the Idaion Antron, the large cave on Mount Ida in Crete, discovered by a shepherd in 1884. These include a host of modelled works in bronze, vases, tripods, sphinxes, shields, weapons, fibulae, goat and bovine figurines. Noteworthy among the exhibits in the case are a restored miniature shield, the bronze bowls, a fibula with incised representation, gold jewellery and the very interesting cut-out sheet no. **11767** showing a man bearing a ram on his shoulders.

Of considerable interest for the cults and ritual practices of the ancient Greeks are the small bronze figurines of Boeotian origin. A large number of these was found in the sanctuary of Apollo on Mount Ptoon, to the east of the drained Lake Kopais, nowadays the extensive fertile plain of Boeotia. Particularly impressive are the tiny animals, mainly bovines, of bronze and lead. Likewise of interest are the horseman no. **13199** and the two sections of a cauldron rim embellished with daedalic figures (no. **7384**).

The astrolabe no. **15087**, which has survived in pieces, is still a mystery in many ways. All we can ascertain is that it consisted of a system of cogwheels and numbered regulae. It was discovered in the sea off Antikythera, together with other antiquities, the most celebrated and significant of which is the so-called Ephebe of Antikythera no. **13396** in gallery 29.

COLLECTION OF SCULPTURES OF THE ROMAN PERIOD

(Rooms 41-43 are temporarily closed).

The period of Roman rule in Greece presents deep and radical difference from the earlier and happier times. The defeat of the Macedonian king Perseus by the Roman consul Aemilius Paulus at Pydna in 168 B.C. (June 22), put an end to Macedonian hegemony and that was the beginning of the end for the Hellenistic kingdoms that had come into being after the death of Alexander the Great. The defeat of the army of the Achaic Commonwealth by the Roman consul Mommius at the Isthmus in 146 B.C. and the ensuing destruction of Corinth, completed the subjugation of Greece.

Greece at the time was an immense museum, its sanctuaries overflowing with exquisite votive offerings. Polyvius reports that there were 2000 works of art in the sanctuary of Apollo at Thermos alone, and that was a relatively unimportant and less frequented sanctuary than the great ones in Delphi or Olympia.

Pillaging of Greece's art treasures began with Aemilius Paulus and continued with the destroyer of Corinth Mommius and the dictator Sylla as leading figures. The denudation of the country, of the sanctuaries and the cities was systematically pursued.

Art, however, did not cease to be cultivated in Greece, though it now lacked the spiritual force of the archaic and the classical periods. Utilitarianism is now the prime factor in every Greek undertaking and is also reflected in art.

Classical art had been marked by the presence of great artists who had created schools. Many names of artists of the Roman period are known but most of their works were insignificant.

Throughout the archaic, classical and hellenistic ages, Greek plastic art had followed a course of unparalleled splendour, had solved all its technical problems and had produced works of art that deserved to be designated as "canons" by the ancients themselves. The philosophical tendencies of the Roman period, always closely associated with artistic trends, now gave particular impetus to the art of portraiture i.e. the art of making likenesses of specific persons.

The art of portraiture in Rome and in Greece had a different spiritual substratum, arising out of each people's different way of thinking. "Behind each individual case, the Greek looks for the general law which the case obeys, whereas the Roman pays attention to the accuracy of detail, classifies the problems and solves them empirically as they arise". This difference is evident between Greek and Roman portraits. When the Greeks portrayed a known personality, say Pericles or Alexander, they would try to put into the likeness all the human properties represented by the person portrayed. They would rather sacrifice complete resemblance of the features if that could only be achieved at the expense of the idealism they wanted to express. For the Romans, on the other hand, absolute likeness was the main concern, so that the early Roman portraits made an impression as if they were copies of wax models of the persons concerned.

In the following rooms, we will see Greek works of the Roman period and we will note that they are still full of the idealism that characterized ancient Greek art. Among the exhibits are several portraits of both Greeks and Romans, which show important differences from corresponding and contemporary works made in Italy. These rooms of the National Museum contain the last reflexion of the superb phenomenon that is classical Greek art.

Room 41, of the statue of Melos

No 244. Statue of a man in himation, of larger-than-life dimensions, from Eretria. The stance is reminiscent of the Hermes of Andros, and of Atalante. The facial features are idealized and there is an expression of sadness. It may have been a funeral statue. The base on which the statue stands is believed to be its own. It bears the following inscription: *Amphicrates Lysandrou to Kleoneikos Lysandrou, his friend.*

No 2800. Portrait of bearded man with tousled hair and band, from Dipylon. The face is wrinkled. Copy of an original of the 1st century B.C. According to one opinion, the person portrayed is the iambic poet Hipponax.

No 340. Portrait of an old man from the Asklepeion of Athens.

No 985. Portrait believed to be the likeness of some poet, possibly Hesiod. Copy of a work of the 3rd or 2nd century B.C.

No 368. Portrait of the philosopher Metrodoros of Lampsakos, a disciple of Epicurus, of the 2nd - 3rd century A.D. Copy of an earlier work of the 3rd century B.C. Formerly, this bust was thought to represent either Epicurus himself or Hermarchos, who was another disciple and his successor.

No 706. Female statue from Thyrea (Loukous monastery), thought to have been an ornament in the villa of the rich sophist Herodes Atticus. It may represent Amymone, daughter of king Danaos, or even Aphrodite.

No 1668. This unfinished funeral statue from Renia, an island near Delos, is of interest, in that it demonstrates the way the sculptors of the Roman period worked.

No 2715. Large equestrian statue of the late 2nd century B.C., from Melos. Despite its many injuries and defects, it is an example of the magnificence of the works that adorned the ancient cities and especially the sanctuaries. The rider wears chiton and himation, as well as a breastplate decorated with a gorgonion bordered by serpents. The left hand held the rein of the horse, while the right was raised.

Room 42, of Cosmetae

No 1828. Statue of naked man, beardless and with clean-shaved head, from Delos. The right hand grasps the chlamys, whose other end is over the left shoulder. It is probably the portrait of a wealthy Roman of the 1st century B.C. Formely believed to represent a flute-player.

No 219. Headless female statue from Andros. It was erected over a grave together with the Hermes No 218, already seen in Room 21. The type of the statue is an imitation of the "Great Herculean". 1st century B.C.

No 3727. Relief from Chalandri, showing Dionysos walking on the left; he holds a scarabee and a thyrsos. Despite its "archaistic" form, it is believed to belong to the 4th century B.C.

No 3625. Bell-shaped marble crater of the 1st century B.C. with decoration in relief on the outside. Below the mouth on the external surface, there is a vine-branch of excellent workmanship; below this, three young girls holding hands, move in

what seems to be a clear though restrained dancing step. The girls — Graces — are copies of 4th century B.C. figures.

No 3758. Portrait of Augustus (27 B.C.-14 B.C.) from the Roman Agora of Athens.

No 3665. Head of Gaius Caesar, grand-son of Augustus, who died in the year 4 A.D., detached from a relief.

No 3606. Portrait of Lucius Caesar, also a grand-son of Augustus; died in the year 2 A.D.

No 430. Portrait of emperor Tiberius (14-37 A.D.).

No 328. Portrait of emperor Claudius (41-54 A.D.), from Smyrna.

No 345. Portrait of emperor Domitianus (81-96 A.D.).

No 1499. Relief from Brauron of Attica, with repressentation of naked Leda being embraced by Zeus in the form of a swan.

The male heads of the hermae in this room have the individual features of actual men (portraits); they were found in 1861, at excavations conducted by the Archaeological Society near Agios Demetrios Katephoris, between the so-called Tower of the Winds and the Acropolis; they were built into the Valerian wall of Athens, but they came originally from a gymnasium which was located in the city, the "Gymnasium of Diogenes", east of the Agora. The 34 hermae found on that occasion make up a real "gallery" as they picture, with the realism of portraits, the officials known as cosmetae; these officials served a one-year term of office, at the end of which the youth of Athens, or the city, honoured them with the erection of such hermae. The hermae are justifiably considered important, as they represent a large sample of the Athenian aristocracy of Roman times. The "cosmetae", elected for one year, were responsible for all aspects of the administration concerning the Athenian ephebes and their office was of the highest importance. Of the many hermae that have come down to us, we will mention only a few: those best preserved or best identified with some persons by their inscriptions.

No 384. Herma with head portraying the cosmete Heliodoros, son of Heliodoros from Piraeus: the wrinkled, beardless face of an old man; on the front side of the herma, there is a number of inscriptions, the first of which is this: "Ἡ ἐξ Ἀρείου Πάγου βουλὴ καὶ ἡ βουλὴ τῶν ἑξακοσίων καὶ ὁ δῆμος ὁ Ἀθηναίων τὸν κοσμητὴν Ἡλιόδωρον (Ἡλιοδώρου) Πειραιέα".

No 387. Herma portraying the cosmete Onasos, son of Palleneus, intact on its original base. It is inscribed with the following epigram: "Λεὼς ἐφήβων τόνδε κοσ | μητὴν θέτο | Ὄνασον Ἑρμάωνι κηδύνας | ἴσον".

No 385. Herma of the cosmete Sosistratos of Marathon. Here he is portrayed as an aged man with thick hair and a short beard; the inscription on the front of the stele mentions the archon of Athens at the time, thereby dating the herma to the year 141/2 or 142/3 A.D.

No 386. Herma of the cosmete Claudius Chrysippos, an aged man with short beard and hair. The first inscription on the front side is this: "Ἑρμῆν Χρυσίππου κοσμήτο | ρος ἐσθλοὶ ἔφηβοι | ἀντ' ἀρετῆς πάσης θῆκαν | ἀριπρεπέως". 142/3 A.D.

Room 43, of Herodes Atticus

The Athenian Herodes Atticus of Marathon (about 101-177 A.D.) was one of the wealthiest men in the ancient world and perhaps the wealthiest in his time; he was a sophist and a great sponsor; as a philosopher, he had a large number of disciples; he was the friend of emperor Hadrian (117-138 A.D.) and of Antoninus (138-161 A.D.), and the tutor of Marcus Aurelius (161-180 A.D.) and of Lucius Verus (161-169 A.D.). Next to nothing has been preserved of his many philosophical writings and no relics of buildings have been positively identified with any of his famous sumptuous villas at Marathon, Kifissia and elsewhere. We do, however, have several likenesses of him, as well as inscriptions from monuments he had sponsored and of likenesses of his friends, especially of his favourite disciple and friend Polydeukion.

The busts No **4810** of Herodes and No **4811** of Polydeukion were found in 1961 in Kifissia, in the general area where Herodes' villa must have stood. The two busts, apart from their excellent state of preservation, are examples of genuine Attic art and they occupy therefore a special place in the series of likenesses of these persons. Found simultaneously at the same site were the horse bust No **4812** and the epicranon No **4813**; the latter, a work of excellent workmanship, is a typical example of the classicism of Hadrian's time, preserving the form but entirely lacking the force and vigour of the genuine classical art it imitates.

No 435. Another head of Herodes Atticus.

No 3729. Head of the Roman emperor Hadrian (117-138 A.D.).

No 249. Bust of emperor Hadrian from the temple of Olympian Zeus. As is well

known, this great temple of Zeus was begun by Peisistratos but was not finished until the 2nd century A.D. when the generosity of Hadrian, who was particularly fond of Athens, allowed it to be completed.

No 449. In Roman times, wives were usually included in the marks of respect paid to great men. This head pictures Sabina, wife of emperor Hadrian.

No 417. A favourite friend and companion of Hadrian's was Antinoos, a young man from Claudiopolis of Bithynia who was famous for his beauty. When Antinoos drowned in the Nile, Hadrian and the Greek cities elevated him to the rank of a demi-god. Statues and busts of him were erected in almost every city and sanctuary in the Greek world, coins imprinted with his likeness were coined, and special rites were introduced in his honour. This bust, found in the typically Roman city of Patras, is a good though cold representation of the beauty of Hadrian's deified favourite.

No 3563. Larger-than-life head of the emperor Antoninus the Pious (138-161 A.D.).

No 572. Head of the emperor Marcus Aurelius (161-180 A.D.).

No 350. Larger-than-life head of a statue of Lucius Verus, co-emperor (161-169 A.D.) with Marcus Aurelius, found in the theatre of Dionysos.

No 263. Statue of Asklepios found in his great sanctuary of Epidaurus in 1886. The god, dressed in a himation, is shown standing, and leaning on a staff wound with the sacred serpent. Beside his left foot there is an omphalos, a symbol of divination befitting Asklepios as the son of Apollo.

130. Male statue No 1828 from Delos, 1st century B.C.

131. Bust of the Athenian sophist Herodes Atticus No 4810 from Kifissia.

132. Bust of Polydeukion, a disciple of Herodes Atticus from Kifissia No 4811.

133. Bust of Antinoos No 417, a friend of Emperor Hadrian.

149

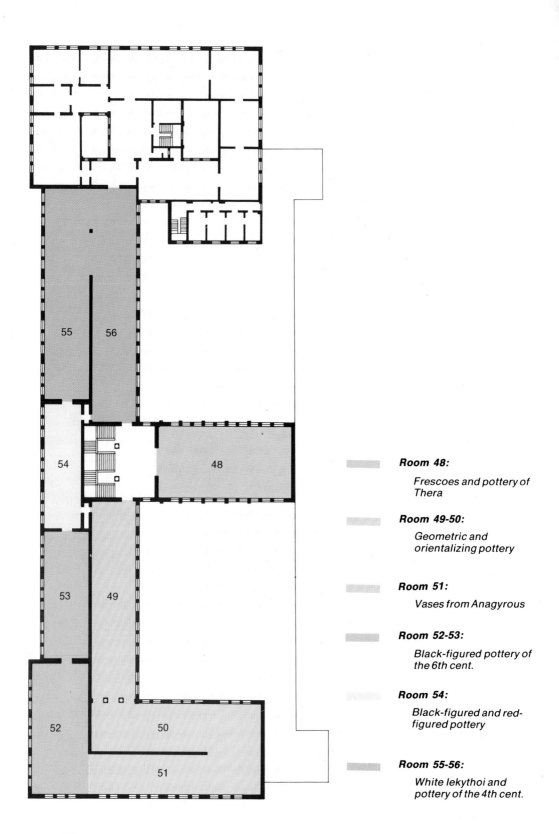

Room 48:

Frescoes and pottery of Thera

Room 49-50:

Geometric and orientalizing pottery

Room 51:

Vases from Anagyrous

Room 52-53:

Black-figured pottery of the 6th cent.

Room 54:

Black-figured and red-figured pottery

Room 55-56:

White lekythoi and pottery of the 4th cent.

THE COLLECTION OF VASES

The history of ceramics runs a parallel course with the history of man. Pottery or pottery fragments found at excavations help archaeologists to draw important conclusions concerning ancient civilizations. But quite apart from their significance as historical documents, ancient Greek vases, especially those of the classical period and those decorated with painting, are often valuable in their own right as works of art.

In the first rooms of the Museum, we saw the neolithic, the Mycenaean, and the Cycladic collections of pottery. In the following rooms, the geometric, archaic, and classical periods of pottery are represented. These exhibits, however, should not be viewed as self-contained entities, but bearing in mind the other forms of art - sculpture, architecture, poetry. The chronological table in the beginning of this book will prove a useful aid.

Room 49. Geometric Pottery

Early Geometric (1000-900 B.C.) and Geometric (900-700 B.C.)

The geometric style, especially as expressed in vase-painting and pottery, has been described as the first monumental achievement of Greek art. The early geometric, preceding the geometric proper style in pottery, shows a sudden change compared with the last period of Mycenaean ceramics. Shapes become more vigorous, contours are more clearly defined and purely geometrical designs are substituted for the "naturalistic" painted decoration of the Mycenaean age.

The amphora (jar with two handles) is the prevalent type of pottery in the early geometric period. It is decorated with black horizontal stripes and semi-circles drawn with compasses; gradually, we find larger parts of the jars painted in black, leaving only a small area free of paint at the shoulder, and this again is decorated with semi-circles, diamonds, combinations of lines, triangles. Though the amphora is prevalent, many other pottery types are current: Oinochoe or wine-pourer, pyxis, calathos, lekythos, skyphos, cup, crater or mixing bowl - all of them articles of everyday use. The black colour of the decorations stands out in contrast with the pale hue of the clay surface.

The creation of early geometric and geometric art has been associated with the Dorians, a view supported by ancient tradition. On the other hand, it has been observed that the best examples of this style were developed in Attica, where the Dorians never set foot.

In both its periods - the early geometric and the geometric proper - the great centre of this style of art was Attica, where geometric pottery culminated in the monumental vases of Dipylon, such as the amphora No 804 we saw in the first room of sculptures. The shapes of the vessels remain essentially the same as those of the early geometric period, but the decoration changes. The black varnish that used to cover the surface of the vases gives way to geometric decorations and representations that spread over increasingly larger areas until they eventually cover the entire surface. In the great funeral amphorae, e.g. No 804, we note meanders - a prevalent design in this period - interlinked diamonds, ellipses, bands of triangles, and a multitude of other ornamental shapes scattered all over and forming frames around representations involving a variety of figures. Shown as a rule in a broad belt is a death or burial scene; the dead person is pictured on a death-bed, surrounded by men holding daggers and by lamenting women. In a second belt on the same vase, the painter would often represent a series of chariots with charioteers, supposed to escort the deceased to the burial place. It is typical of the style that, other than the main figures in the scenes, the representations are full of geometric ornamental designs such as swastikas, dotted rosettes, dots, wavy lines, even animal forms e.g. duck and antelope.

Human figures - naked men and women, sometimes with the breasts indicated in the latter - are shadowy. To show the facial features, the area inside the contour of the head is left unpainted, then a dot is made to indicate, say, an eye. The chest is triangular, the legs are elongated, spidery.

Painted figures and ornamental designs are always strictly symmetrical in their arrangement, in accord with the perfect shape of the vase.

Show-case 2: Early geometric vases from a cemetery of Nea Ionia near Athens. No **16362** and **16363:** Women's jewellery - broaches and pins; No **18115,** early geometric amphora with serrated decoration at the rounded part of the body and at the neck. The rest of the vase is covered with black; the vigorous and dynamic shape is enhanced by the scant decoration.

Show-case 3: The exhibits in this case, found in graves of the area around the Arios Pagos, are some of the earliest geometric vessels discovered in Athens. No **15314,** oinochoe (wine-pourer) with clover-shaped mouth, made up of superposed successive vases; No **15318,** pyxis with cap ornamented with molded bull-head.

Show-case 4: Geometric vases, jewels and toys from the Eleusis grave known as "grave of Isis", so called on account of the miniature figurine of that goddess, No **10963** found in it. In the same case, vases found in Megara but made in Corinth.

Show-case 5: Geometric vases. Of particular interest are the large crater fragments No **802** with death scene including mourners, warriors armed with spears and figure-of-eight shields, and chariot race.

Show-case 13: Attic geometric vases, donated by G. Empedokles. The same shapes and scenes can be seen in the other show-cases in this Room.

Base No 806. Large geometric crater with representation of chariot race.

Show-case 6: Vases of the mature stage of the geometric style: Nos **169, 186, 201, 202,** come from the Athenian grave near the Pnyx. Much appreciated for its shape and decoration is the small oinochoe No **152,** attributed to the "painter of Dipylon"; the body is decorated with black bands, the shoulder is all black, the neck is painted with a grazing antelope. The simple decoration of this small vase contrasts pleasantly with the other, richly decorated, vases of the same period. About 750 B.C.

Show-case 7-8: Geometric vases from graves in Piraeus street, explored in the last century. The fragments No **802** showing war scenes with several persons, and likenesses of ships, and No **812,** showing a death-scene are worthy of note.

Show-case 9-10: Geometric vessels from graves (?) in Piraeus street. No **802,** fragments of large vessels representing warriors; No **184,** amphora with representation of chariot race.

Show-case 11: An excavation carried out on Mt. Hymettus many years ago (1935), revealed a sanctuary of Zeus Ombrios. Found in that sanctuary were many vase fragments engraved with some of the earliest Attic inscriptions and therefore important for the study of Attic script. No **192,** small late geometric oinochoe, with engraved the most ancient Attic inscription reading from right to left, on the shoulder: *"Ηος νυν ορχεστον παντον αταλοτατα παιζει, τοτοδεκλλμιν"*. This oinochoe was found in 1871 in a grave, possibly near the Kerameikos, and is dated to the second half of the 8th century B.C.

Show-case 12: The two small clay heads No **4382** and **4381,** represent the earliest beginnings of Greek sculpture. They were found at Amyclaeon, at a distance of some 7 km from Sparta, at the site of the sanctuary of Apollo, which contained the celebrated "throne" of that god, made by Bathykles around 500 B.C. The former head (4382) dates from the Mycenaean period. The facial features are indicated with paint on the whitish clay plaster. The other head (4381), which is geometric and therefore much later, contrasts sharply with the first in both shape and size; No **148,** geometric vase (pyxis) with molded little horses on the cap; No **16351,** little bronze geometric horse; No **17973,** geometric pyxis with three molded little horses on the cap.

Base No 811. Large geometric oinochoe with molded bird on cap; the entire body is covered with geometric designs except a belt on the rounded part which is decorated with a row of antelopes.

Show-case 14: Vases of the late geometric period, from Anabyssos, Attica. Of interest is cyathos No **14477** showing a dancing scene, and cylix **14475** with two lions tearing a mannikin to pieces.

Base No 18062. Large geometric amphora with two illustrated belts: On the upper belt, death scene with mourning women; on the lower belt, procession of warriors armed with swords and spears, their bodies covered with large figure-of-eight shields. Middle 8th century B.C.

Base No 803. This amphora from Dipylon is a monumental work, matching the one seen in the first room of sculptures and decorated by the same painter. This vase of impressive size and shape epitomizes the features of mature Attic geometric pottery.

Room 50. Geometric and Orientalizing Pottery

Orientalizing pottery: The vigorous geometric pottery so successfully developed mainly in Attica, was succeeded by the so-called orientalizing pottery, whose main centre was Corinth. Thanks to its privileged geographical position between two seas, this important city maintained busy trade activities with both east and west. One branch of the new style, known as "Ionic" developed in Asia Minor and in the Aegean islands and exercised direct influence on Egypt and Italy; it produced excellent works in Rhodes (pottery with animal and floral decoration), in Chios (also known as Naucration art), Clazomenae, Laconia a.o.

The orientalizing pottery of Corinth introduces the silhouetting technique by engraving, later continued in the black-figured Attic style. The themes are again animals - panthers, lions, double animals with one head, as well as narrative representations of mythological subjects. Corinthian pottery was short-lived, phasing out in about 550 B.C. Athenian competition and the higher quality of Attic vases drove it completely out of the market.

Base No 990. Large geometric crater from Dipylon, painted with burial scene (the dead body is in the carriage surrounded by naked mourning women and men armed with swords). A chariot race is pictured lower, in a second belt. The rest of the vase is covered with linear geometric designs and wide brownish-black bands.

134. *Large geometric funerary crater No 990 from Dipylon.*

135. *Large geometric funerary amphora No 804.*

136. *Scene of laying-out of dead depicted on funerary amphora No 804.*

Show-case 17: Geometric vases donated by G. Empedokles: No **18458,** two clay wheels from carriage replica; No **18520** and **18528,** pyxides with three horses on the caps. No **18140,** cyathos set with representation of tripods supporting cauldrons. The tripod, an object held particularly valuable in Homeric times, is a characteristic offering to Apollo, witness the fine large bronze tripods found in Olympia or in Delphi. No **18135,** amphora with decorated neck, showing a tripod between two horses.

Show-case 18: Attic vases of the early orientalizing style, so-called "proto-Attic" of the first half of the 7th century B.C.; No **14538,** proto-Attic oinochoe; the mouth is clover-shaped, while the cap is decorated with anthemions hanging on branches; second half of the 7th century B.C.; No **332,** proto-Attic oinochoe with clover-shaped mouth; on the cap, head of lionness, wearing the fierce expression popular to the artists of that period. Middle 7th century B.C.

Show-case 20: Vases of the geometric and late geometric period, made in Boeotia and Laconia. The clay cart loaded with pottery No **14481,** from Euboea is interesting; No **12896,** crater from Boeotia, richly illustrated with armed men and horses.

Base No 220. Amphora from Boeotia; the main representation shows the mistress of game, i.e. a winged goddess usually flanked by two lions, which she sometimes holds. This theme, with minor differences, is first encountered in Crete and in Mycenaean Greece. 7th century B.C.

Base No 17762. Attic jar from the Schliemann collection; warrior departing on chariot, wife with infant bidding him farewell. This scene is a common theme in vase-painting. In the lower part of the vase, a belt of animals. 7th century B.C.

Base No 313. The "hydria of Analatos", so-called from the place of its discovery near Athens; about 700 B.C. The geometric designs decorating the lower part of the vase, fairly sophisticated ones, coexist with purely orientalizing forms. The upper part of the body is decorated with lions showing vigorous movement, and with birds and plants characterized by a different spirit than the strictly geometric concept; on the neck, men and women hold hands while performing some kind of religious dance to the music of the lyre. On the perforated handle, as well as on the horizontal handles of the vase, molded serpents (chthonic symbols) clearly indicate the funeral purpose of the hydria.

Small show-case on the wall, No 19. Vases made in Corinthian workshops; a series of these demonstrates the evolution of the Corinthian "aryballos" in the 7th century B.C.; No **18595,** small, pear-shaped aryballos, with likeness of a horseman proceeding towards the left.

Show-case 21: Boeotian vases and figurines of the geometric and the orientalizing period; No **249,** Cylix from a Boeotian workshop, with decoration of anthemions separated by vertical stripes of ornamental designs; middle 6th century B.C.; No **19764,** "calathos" from a Boeotian workshop, decorated with anthemions and birds. Middle 6th century B.C.

Show-case 22: Clay figurines of the 7th century, from Boeotia; No **4017,** man on horseback; details shown in black; spirited expression on the animal's head; No **13257,** richly decorated figurine of goddess seated on throne; the "pole" of the goddess is set with molded rosettes and swastikas.

Show-case 23. No 276, pyxis with representation of dogs; No **4009,** figurine of woman with richly painted dress; No **12995,** figurine of dog; perforated paws suggest that it was fitted with wheels, probably to be used as a toy; painted decoration on forehead.

Room 51. Vases from Anagyron

Early Attic (proto-Attic) style: As pointed out earlier, the geometric style flourished in Attica; in its later stages, however, it showed considerable development in several other Greek areas, such as the Cyclades (800-700 B.C.), Crete and Rhodes (750-650 B.C.), and especially in Corinth where, during the last phase of geometric pottery, the style underwent a transformation and became the early Corinthian black-figured type of pottery.

In Attica, when the geometric style was abandoned, a new type, the so-called *early Attic pottery* which was to produce many outstanding works (710-600 B.C.) appeared on the scene; its evolution was extremely rapid; its culminating point is represented by the black-figured amphora of Nessos No 1002, black figures painted on the light-coloured background, dating from abt. 615 B.C., of a size that competes with that of geometric ware. The early Attic style is the link between Attic geometric pottery and the black-figured pottery of the 6th century. Works of this style, showing excellent craftsmanship, have been found in the cemeteries of Kerameikos in Athens, of Anagyron in the modern area of Vari in Attica, and of Aegina. The "hydria of Analatos" we saw earlier (Room 50, No 313), is the first step towards the new style: geometric and orientalizing elements coexisting in the same work. In the course of the 7th century, the craftsmen of Attica will produce outstanding examples of this style, the engraving technique introduced by Corinthian artists will become generalized, and Attic vases will become replete with oriental and mythical animals - lions, panthers, Chimeras, Pegasus - before going on the mythological scenes, such as the scene depicted on the vase of Nessos, the work of one of the most outstanding painters of the new style, the so-called "painter of Nessos". The early Attic style was for Athenian craftsmen a period of apprenticeship before they could achieve the perfection of the black-figured style which was going to make them the undisputed masters in both the artistic and in the commercial sphere.

Show-case 24-27: Vases and figurines of the orientalizing style from the Aegean islands (Paros, Thera, Rhodes, Samos, Crete, Thassos) and from Cyprus. 7th century B.C. No **17874,** base of vase from Thassos, with engraved tripods, sphinxes, tritons, pegasus; No **12717,** oinochoe from Rhodes showing six chamois (lower belt), birds and deer (upper belt). This oinochoe is believed to have been decorated by two painters: one did the shoulder and part of the rounded portion, the other painter did the rest. No **12718,** oinochoe from Rhodes with a similar representation.

Base No 911. Amphora from Melos, famous for the painting on it: on a chariot drawn by winged horses, Apollo, holding the lyre, accompanies two hyperborian virgins or Muses; standing in the front is his sister Artemis with bow and arrows, her right hand holding a deer by the horns. Pictured on the neck of the vase are Achilles and Memnon in duel; the latter was the son of Eo and Tithon (nephew of Priam, king of Troy), and as we know from Homer, he was defeated in that duel. This amphora is a specimen of a particular variety - the Melian variety - of orientalizing pottery, and one of its characteristics is the excessive use of auxiliary decorations; rosettes, swastikas, anthemions, spirals, cover every bit of available space. Abt. 640 B.C.

Base 28. Amphorae made in Eretria in the 7th century B.C. No **12077,** decorated with three figures on the neck, and lions on the body of the vase; No **12129,** the same representation shown on the neck, while a sphinx adorns the body.

Show-case 31: Vases and figurines of the orientalizing style from Aegina, Boeotia, and Attica. The clay slab No **11119** was found in the sanctuary of Apollo on Mt. Ptoon of Boeotia and is engraved with an archaic epigram to Apollo, dating from the early 6th century B.C.; the epigram is typical of that period's reverent attitude toward the gods: A fine statue I, for the far-throwing king Apollo made by Damosidas Echestrotos and sent by..., whom thou, lord, keep and give them honour and wealth.

Base No 16384. Amphora from Tumulus A of Anagyron, Attica, dated about 620 B.C., showing Prometheus in chains on Mt. Caucasus, and Herakles aiming an arrow at the eagle who devoured Prometheus' liver.

Show-case 29: Vases from Tumulus A of the great cemetery of Anagyron. The main themes are sphinxes, lions, boars and chimaeras.

Show-case 30: Vases from the same tumulus as above. No **16353,** bowl with two handles, decorated with sphinx, boar, panther, lion and a he-goat. No **16391,** black-figured amphora with representations on both sides: Bellerephont on Pegasus, the winged horse with whose help he will kill Chimaera, the latter being shown on the other side of the vase; this mythical monster was part lion with a serpent's tail and part goat; its mouth spat flames. It is shown here with its head turned back. The open mouth with the hideous teeth are a mark of the artist's imagination. Late 7th century B.C.

Show-case 32: Vase from tumulus A of Anagyron.

Show-case 34: Vessels representing the earliest stage of the black-figured style, later to become a commanding influence chronological and geographic as well as in artistic terms: No **903, 16401, 16402:** Partly preserved amphorae decorated with horse' busts in metopes. No **16380:** small amphora with boar representation; a female head is pictured on the neck.

Base No 1002. This is the vase known as "amphora of Nessos": shown on the neck of the vase is Herakles (inscr. HERAKLES) while he kills the centaur Nessos (inscr. NETOS) - a scene illustrating a well-known legend concerning this hero; on the rounded part of the body, a scene from the legend of Medusa who is killed by Perseus, is depicted: Medusa is already dead and beheaded, and her two hideous sisters, Stheno and Eureale, with their brazen claws and their golden wings, are in hot pursuit of Perseus. According to the legend, so powerful was their glance, that they turned into stone whomever they looked at. The Attic artist has been able to bring alive with unique force the ancients' beliefs about the Gorgons: they are flying with furious speed - the bent legs were a conventional way of creating the impression of speed; the belt with the dolphins under their feet indicates that they are flying over the sea; the dolphins are deliberately pointed in the opposite direction, to increase by contrast the sense of the Gorgons' quick flight.

The black-figured amphora of Nessos was found in a grave in the area of Athens; despite some elements borrowed from Corinthian pottery, it is a genuinely Attic work and represents a great step in the direction of pure black-figured style, which was soon to produce unique masterpieces.

Room 52, Black-figured Attic pottery of the 6th century

Black-figured Attic pottery (600-480 B.C.): The legislative and economic measures enacted by Solon to enable the city of Athens to overcome its social problems did much to improve the situation of small tradesmen and craftsmen and were largely responsible for the new impetus of Attic pottery, which until that time had been suppressed by Corinthian competition.

The amphora of Nessos was illustrated by an unknown painter conventionally referred to as "the painter of Nessos". An equally unknown painter, a disciple of the former, has come to be known as "the painter of Gorgon" on account of a celebrated work of abt. 600 B.C., now in the Louvre. Represented in this Museum is a later painter, named Sophilos. Sophilos was followed by the vase-painter Klitias, whose most famous work is the "François vase"; another known vase-painter was the Lydian Exekias, also known as "the painter of Amasis", who had formed a small artistic group and excelled in miniature painting.

137. The famous amphora of Nessos No 1002, an important work of early Attic ceramic.
138. Melian amphora No 911 showing Apollo on chariot and a duel of warriors.

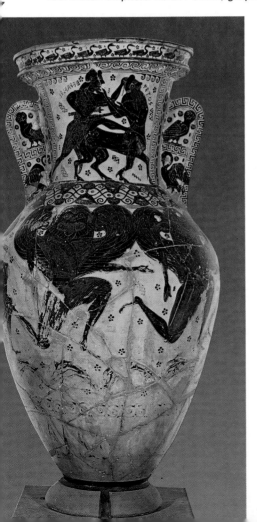

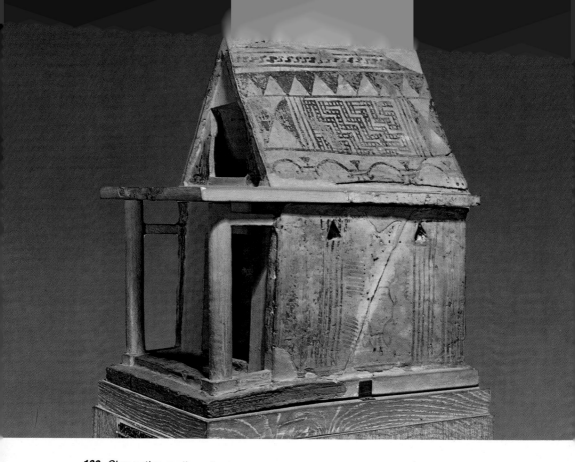

139. Clay votive replica of a house or temple No 15471, *from the Heraeon of Argos, late geometric period.*

In the black-figured style, the figures are black, and their features, anatomy, clothing etc. are indicated by engraved lines. The background is the natural colour of clay, i.e. the material from which the vase is made. Occasionally, white or purple colour is used to enhance certain points.

Around 530 B.C., a new style in vase-painting, the red-figured type, strikes a terrible blow at black-figured painting. The change is evident in the quality of the painters rather than in the quantity of production, which remains profuse at least until 500 B.C.

At an approximate distance of 9 km from Argos, there are the ruins of a great sanctuary dedicated to Hera, which was the national sanctuary of the Argives. It was explored between 1892 and 1895 by the American School of Archaeology under Ch. Waldstein, and later by others. In ancient times, this was a famous and highly respected sanctuary; it was there that Agamemnon accepted the oath of the Achaean leaders prior to their departure for Troy. The excavations brought to light a multitude of relics spanning the entire antiquity, from the Mycenaean to the Roman period.

In Room 17, of sculpture, we saw the head of Hera No 1571, fragments of metopes and other sculptural and architectural members of the temple. Displayed in the show-cases in this Room, are small art objects that are of great value for the knowledge of the history of the sanctuary.

Show-cases 35-37: Standing out from the variety of relics of Hera's sanctuary exhibited, are the vases - Mycenaean, geometric, early Corinthian and orientalizing;

the clay and bronze figurines of the same periods; the jewels (broaches, clasps etc.); the clay and bronze figurines of the archaic and classical periods.

Show-case 46: Fragments of pottery by "the painter of the Gorgons". This painter, a disciple of "the painter of Nessos", has a predilection for animals, which he paints in symmetrical groups. Sophilos, the first painter of black-figured pottery known to us by name (in show-case 42 we came across Timonidas, the only known Corinthian painter), follows the style of the "painter of Gorgon". Fragment No **15499** from a black-figured "dinos" found in Pharsala, Thessaly, shows a chariot race conducted in Troy in honour of the memory of Patroclus. The scene is inspired by the verses 259 ff of Book Ψ of the Iliad where Achilles, to hounour his dead friend,

and made them to sit in a wide gathering;
and from his ships brought forth prizes; cauldrons and tripods
and horses and mules and strong oxen
and fair-girdled women and grey iron.
(transl by A.T. Murray).

On the left we see the four horses of a chariot (the first is white in order to stand out), and on the right there is a wooden platform with a gesticulating crowd, absorbed by the race. In the middle, written in colour by the vase-painter, is the inscription: "Painted by Sophilos: races in honour of Patroclus"; on the right, the name Ἀχιλὲς (Achilles) pointed to the hero who had organized the games. No **15165,** fragment of "dinos" picturing the wedding of Peleus and Thetis.

A particular class of vases in this show-case are those depicting "komastae" i.e. revellers: they are mainly cylices or skyphoi, shapes borrowed from Corinth, and the figures they represent are usually naked or lightly dressed and engaged in spirited dancing. No **940** shows a dancing man and a youth, a flute-player and a youth, while No **528,** a skyphos, pictures two dancing men, both works of the same painter. Skyphos No **640** represents a man with a lyre, and youths and men with jugs full of wine.

Show-case 47: Black-figured vases of the early 6th century B.C. No **12587,** crater by Sophilos, depicting Herakles wrestling with Nereus; No **991,** "loutrophoros" by the same painter with belts of animals.

Show-case 48: Black-figured pottery of Boeotia, and clay figurines. No **4082,** clay quadriga with two warriors. Nos **4021-4030,** clay spoons with handles shaped like animal heads - calf, hen, hare, horse - with the features of the animals painted, and various geometric designs in the hollow of the spoon. No **12218,** slab-shaped aryballos inscribed with: *"Μνασάλκες ποίεσε"* (made by Mnasalkes).

Show-case 39. From Hera's temple in Argos: Of particular interest are the two clay tablets No **14210** and **14214** showing in relief the figure of Aristaeos, son of Apollo and of the Nymph Kyrene, a deity connected with agriculture and vegetation. No **14016,** bronze tablet from the Heraeon of Argos, engraved with a law, dated 575-550 B.C.

No 17870. Clay trunk of sphinx serving as an acroterium in the temple of Artemis Laphria at Kalydon of Aetolia, a striking work of Corinthian art.

Base No 15471. Clay votive replica of a temple (or house) with posts from the Heraeon of Argos: late geometric period (around 680 B.C.) with orientalizing elements. A number of temples of this simple votive design have been found in Greece.

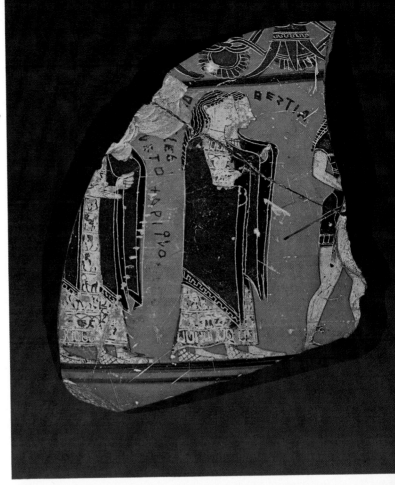

142

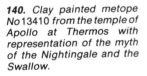

140. *Clay painted metope No 13410 from the temple of Apollo at Thermos with representation of the myth of the Nightingale and the Swallow.*

141. *Wooden painted panel No 16464 from the area of Sicyon, showing preparation of a lamb.*

142. *Fragment of dinos No 15165 with remains of a scene from the wedding of Peleus and Thetis.*

143. *Fragment of dinos No 15499 preserving part of a representation of a chariot race, a work of the vase painter Sophilos.*

Base No 16684. Geometric replica of small house, from Perachora; it includes an arch and has a curved roof decorated with imprinted triangles. There are posts in front, and before these, there are twin columns on a rectangular base.

At some distance (32 km) from the Isthmus of Corinth, lies the site Perachora; two sanctuaries were explored there by the English School of Archaeology: one of *Hera Akraea,* and one of *Hera Limenia.* The excavation produced many valuable finds, the most important of which are exhibited here.

Show-case 40 (on the wall): Objects from Perachora and from the Heraeon of Argos: No **16524,** ivory tablet with representation. No **16520,** small ivory male head. No **16519,** small ivory round sphinx. No **15131,** bronze plaque from the Heraeon of Argos used as lining for a wooden piece of furniture, with molded representation of the murder of Cassandra by Clytemnestra; the ill-fated daughter of Priam, king of Troy and of Hecube, had been taken by Agamemnon, as a spoil, to Mycenae, where she was to die with him.

Show-case 43: The exhibits in this case are offerings connected with the worship of Hera at Perachora; they include bronze vases, figurines, clasps a.o. On the calf No **16156** there is a votive inscription saying: *"Ναυμάχος μὲ ἀνέθηκε τᾶ "Ηρα τᾶ Λιμενία"* (I was dedicated by Naumachos to Hera Limenia). No **16183,** arm (hand) from large bronze statue.

Show-case 49: The number of offerings dedicated to Hera at Perachora was incredibly large; these are some of them, including early Corinthian and Corinthian vases, figurines, sculptured vessels, ivory tablets with a variety of representations. 7th and 6th century B.C. The clay tablet No **16477** shows a likeness of the Aristaeon (see case 39).

Show-case 41: Corinthian vases: No **625,** "mastos", unusual skyphos-like vase, its lower part shaped like a female breast (Greek = mastos), decorated with figures of revellers. No **3929, 10778,** sculptured vases in rabbit form.

Show-case 42: Corinthian pottery: Of special importance is vase No **277,** painted by *Timonidas,* the only Corinthian painter we know by name. Pictured on the vase, which dates from about 580 B.C., is a scene of the killing of Troilos, son of the king of Troy Priam, by Achilles. On the right-hand side of the picture, the heavily armed Achilles hides behind a tree near the fountain (the water flows out of a bronze lion-head); Polyxene, a sister of Troilos' known from the epic poetry of Cyprus, is filling a water jug, and Troilos is approaching from behind her to water the horses; on the left-hand side Priam is shown, although tradition has him absent from the scene, in order to make the representation more easily understandable to the viewer. Painted in front of Achilles (scarcely legible) is the painter's signature: *"Τιμωνίδας μ' ἔγραψε"* (I was painted by Timonidas), where the vase is speaking on behalf of the painter. There are also inscriptions mentioning the names of all the characters, including the horses. But the colours have faded and the representation is now hardly visible.

Show-case 44: In Sparta, on the hill north of the ancient theatre, the ruins of the sanctuary of Athena Chalkioikos (Athena who lives in a bronze house), were explored in 1907. It was here, in the temple of the goddess, that the king of Sparta Pausanias died in 477 B.C. when the Ephores walled in the openings shutting him inside. At a small distance from the town, near the river Eurotas, another sanctuary, that of Artemis Orthia was explored in 1906. The two sanctuaries yielded a wealth of finds, most of which are in the museum of Sparta. Exhibited here are some of the most important, including bronze statuettes and ivory objects with representations. 7th-6th century B.C.

Showcase - table 45: At the site Pitsa, west of Sicyon near the Gulf of Corinth, a cave explored in 1934 produced many offerings to the Nymphs, dating from the 7th century B.C. The most important of them were four small paintings on wood (Nos 16464-67), with decorations which consist the unique samples of Corinthian painting in the 6th century B.C. The artist first covered the wood board with a white layer and then painted with tempera. Painting No **16464,** its bright colours well preserved, represents a lamb sacrifice. Standing before the altar, a woman holds a pourer in her right hand, using the left to steady a tray containing the paraphernalia of the sacrifice, which she carries on her head. Behind her are three children: the first brings the tied lamb, the second plays the lyre and the third plays the double flute. They are followed by two women carrying branches; another branch visible behind them was probably carried by further woman. All are crowned with myrtle wreaths and are wearing red himations, with the exception of the child with the lyre, and embroidered blue chitons. Over the figures, to the right, there is a votive inscription in archaic Corinthian script: *[--άν] έθεκε ταῖς Ν[ύ]νφαις [--]ο qορίνθιος* (Dedicated to the Nymphes by ..., Corinthian). The names of the two women on the left are *Euthydika* and *Eukolis.* This indicates that the painting had been made to order and that the names refer to actual persons. About 540 B.C. No **16465,** painting on wood, showing women separated by their postures into two groups; they are festively dressed with colourful chitons and himations covering their heads, and they are crowned with golden wreaths. Their names are saved in inscriptions over their heads. Beside the woman in the red himation, the name "Telessio" appears in Corinthian script. Late 6th century B.C. Nos **16466** and **16467:** These paintings, too, show women in scenes connected with the worship of the Nymphs in the cave, but they are less well preserved.

The paintings in the showcase are not the originals which, on account of their condition, have to be kept in a specially air-conditioned environment; they are copies made by E. Gillieron fils.

Show-case 50: Offerings from the sanctuary of Artemis Orthia in Sparta, made of ivory and bone; most are productions of local workshops and they date from the 7th and 6th century B.C. Of considerable interest is the ivory relief No **15362** with the likeness of a war ship (the oarsmen are armed) and a woman bidding them farewell on the left. Late 7th century B.C. No **15368,** ivory comb with representation of the judgment of Paris. Late 7th century B.C. The lead figurines showing Artemis as "mistress of game" come from the *Menelaion* (sanctuary of Menelaus and Helen near Sparta).

Painted metopes from the temple of Apollo Thermios Not far from the village Thermos of Aetolia are the ruins of the sanctuary of Apollo Thermios, which belonged to the Aetolian Commonwealth and was destroyed twice, in 218 and 206 B.C., respectively, by Philip V, of Macedonia. These painted clay metopes of the late 7th century B.C. come from the third temple of Apollo at Thermos. They are the only remains of large archaic paintings; they show the direct influence of Corinthian vase painting, but are inferior in the composition of their themes. The following metopes can be seen from left to right: No **13413,** metope picturing two women. No **13401,** metope showing Perseus in flight (in direction to the right) after killing Medusa. An episode of this myth was seen in the amphora of Nessos. No **13402,** metope with gorgonion, a popular theme in vase and other painting. No **13410,** metope with two women bending over a table where a child is lying - an episode from the myth of the Swallow and the Nightingale (Aedon and Chelidon); painted on the right is the name of the one Χελιδϝόν (Chelidon). In the Attic version of the myth, they are called Prokne and Philomela; Prokne's husband Tereus, king of Thrace, raped Prokne's sister Philomela; to punish him, Prokne slaughtered their son Itys, and served him to Tereus as a meal; when he realized what had happened, Tereus wanted to kill the two women, but the gods intervened transforming Tereus into a heath-cock, Prokne into a swallow and Philomela into a nightingale. No **13409,** metope representing a hunter with boar and deer hanging on pole. No **13407,** another metope with three goddesses seated in thrones, seen from the side, one partly covering the other.

Room 53, Black-figured pottery of the 6th century B.C.

Show-case 51: Black-figured vases from Anagyron (Vari): No **19163,** black-figured urn (lekythos), by the "painter of Amasis". No **19177,** bowl, with mourning female figure on each handle. No **19171,** black-figured Attic plate with representation of running Gorgon, legs in striding motion, wings outspread, lotus-flowers around the edge. Late 7th cent. B.C.

Show-case 52: Small objects, such as figurines, pebbles, jewels, sealstones, most interesting of which are those coming from the sanctuaries of Sounion. No **14935,** clay tablet showing ship and soldiers from the sanctuary of Athena Sounias, dating from the 7th century B.C. approximately; the soldiers are armed with spear and shields; helmsman sitting in the rear.

Show-case 59: Black-figured pottery: urns, wine-pourers, plates, skyphoi. No **18880,** plate fragment from the Acropolis with representation of Herakles wrestling with Kyknos, son of Ares, a work of the "Lydian painter". No **507,** plate by the same painter showing Achilles receiving his weapons from his mother Thetis; mentioned beside each figure is its name. No **404,** black-figured urn from Tanagra; represented is Helen with her brothers, the Dioscuri Castor and Pollux conducting her back to Sparta after her abduction by Theseus, by the painter of Amasis. About 530 B.C.

Base No 606: Black-figured Attic "dinos" by the "painter of 606", as its painter has been conventionally named. In the upper belt, dense representation of Homeric battle, as deduced from the chariots accompanying the combattants; decorative belt in the middle, and, below, again a battle scene between Greek horsemen and Asian fighters. From the Acropolis, about 570-560 B.C.

Show-case 60: Corinthian and Attic vases of the first half of the 6th century B.C., mainly cylices. No **1104,** cylix of the so-called "micro-artist" type. No **559,** the "amphora of Olympus", believed to be one of the earliest Panathenian amphorae, before 566 B.C. (which is the year when athletic competitions were added to the Panathenian Games); the vase shows two men listening to a flute-player; the latter may be Olympus, the legendary son (or father) of the satyr Marcyas, the famous competitor of Apollo in the flute-playing contest (see related relief of Mantineia in Room 30); shown on the other side of the amphora is a horseman with his groom; about 570 B.C. No **529,** the "cylix of Ross" from the name of the German archaeologist, showing Herakles and the centaur Nessos on the inside, and a chariot race on the outside. No **992,** Corinthian cylix with two women in profile shown on the inside, over their heads are the names Nevris and Klyka; the clearly indicated contours enhance the figures of the girls, who are depicted in a reverential

144

145

144-145. Black-figured vessels from the cemetery of Anagyron, of the 6th century B.C. (case 51).

144. *Oinochoe No 19176 with representation of bull and lion; rosettes fill the background between the figures.*

145. *Oinochoe No 19159 with likeness of Hermes holding the caduceus and wearing winged sandals; with sphinxes to the right and left; a decorative frieze can be seen over the figures.*

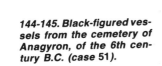

attitude; pictured on the outside are Homeric battles, and scenes with revellers. 590-575 B.C.

Show-case 57, No 1055, black-figured aryballos showing men and women with a sphinx and a gorgonion. At the base, there is the inscription: *"Κεάλτες ἔγραφσεν Μνησ[ικλε]ίδης ἔδοκεν Φοκί".* Middle of 6th century B.C.

Show-case 53: Exhibits from Lemnos: clay god figurines, small house replicas, black-figured vases.

Show-case 54, of Etruria: black-figured vases with representations in relief and engraved decorations.

Nos 13427 and 13939. Two clay sarcophagi from Klazomenae. This city, situated on the southern part of the Gulf of Smyrna, flourished in the 7th and 6th century B.C.; it was known for its lucrative business in clay sarcophagi. The decorations are representative of the themes commonly used by artists in Asia Minor. The first sarcophagus is set with ornamental designs such as anthemions, and with charriot racing and fighting scenes; ornamental designs and animals are prevalent in the other.

Show-case 61: Fragments of black-figured vases by the painters Lydos, Klitias, Nearchos, the painter of Amasis, from the excavation of the Acropolis of Athens. An excellent work is No **15166** by Nearchos, a cantharus fragment showing Achilles in front of three horses yoked to his chariot. The fragment demonstrates the possibilities of engraving as used in the black-figured style as well as the skill of the artist. About 560 B.C.

Show-case 58: A special place in Greek pottery belongs to the pottery developed in the Greek islands in the 6th century B.C. The vases and other objects in this show-case represent such insular pottery, especially from Samos and Rhodes workshops. No **2072** a.o.: vases in the shape of sandal-wearing feet. No **2074, 14849:** small molded vessels in the shape of helmeted heads. No **16004:** cover with representation of Bellerephont on Pegasus. No **1944:** cover with representation of Chimaera.

Show-case 62: Black-figured Attic vases, craters, amphorae, cylices. No **1007:** amphora from Eretria with representation of two warriors in large metope on the rounded part. No **15111:** black-figured amphora with two fighting warriors.

Show-case 55, from Klazomenae of Asia Minor. Black-figured and orientalizing vases. No **16100:** fragment showing Priam and Hecube, or god and goddess, seated on throne.

Unnumbered: Crater from Pharsala, Thessaly, possibly from the workshop of Exekias, with representation of battle around the dead body of Patroclus on one side, and Dionysos surrounded by satyrs on the other.

Show-case 63: Black-figured Attic vases: urns, wine-pourers, water-jugs, plates. Of particular importance are the fragments of black-figured paintings of death scenes from graves: No **2413+2410:** representation of a procession of mourners with raised arms. No **12697:** fragments of paintings showing men and women mourners. No **2414-2417:** these four fragments are from a painting by the great painter in the black-figured tradition, Exekias. These clay plaques are also very informative as they demonstrate otherwise unknown details of funeral ceremonies.

Room 54. Black-figured and red-figured pottery

Attic red-figured pottery (530-320 B.C.). While the various vase-painting styles succeed one another without break and in close interdependence since we find, at least in the beginning of each style, many of the earlier elements coexisting with the new, red-figured pottery seems to have sprung up overnight around 530 B.C. without any connection at all with the black-figured. It was the invention of an unknown painter, named the "painter of Andokides", a disciple of Exekias who appears to have influenced the work of the master.

The red-figured style is the exact reverse of the black-figured. In the red-figured style, the figures are outlined with fine black lines on the unpainted surface of the vase, and the background is covered with black, enhancing the light-coloured figures. The new technique allows the painter greater freedom and enables him to work faster than was possible with the engraving process of the black-figured style.

The period between 530 and 480 B.C. is the so-called "strict style" period of red-figured pottery and is represented by outstanding painters including the "painter of Andokides", Psiakas, Oltos, the great Euphronios, Euphthimides, Smikros, Epiktetos, Douris, a.o. The archaic influences still visible during this period disappear in the following, so-called "free-style" period (480-380 B.C.), which is dominated by the "painter of Pan", the "painter of Penthesilia", Hermonax, the "painter of Achilles".

The 4th century B.C. is the period of decline of Attic red-figured pottery. A new type, the "Kerts style", appears around 370 B.C., flourishes in the decade 350-340 B.C. and disappears suddenly.

Show-case 64: Black-figured Attic lekythoi: No **1125:** Representation of Amphiaraos, one of the "Seven Against Thebes", sinking into the earth; about 490 B.C. No **12947:** clay "loutrophoros" with representation of death-scene.

Show-case 65: Black-figured urns, cylices and oinochoae from Attica: No **1133:** urn showing the sorceress Circe with the companions of Odysseus transformed into swine. No **1132:** black-figured urn; Herakles supports the celestial vault on his shoulders, while Atlas presents him with the apples of the Hesperides.

Show-case 73: Vases and clay figurines from Attic and Boeotian workshops of the 6th century B.C.: No **432:** Boeotian cantharus showing the hunt of the Caledonian Boar; the dogs fall upon the wounded beast; on the right the Amazon Atalante. Represented on the other side of the vase are galloping horses with riders. About 550 B.C.

Show-case 74: Black-figured urns from Attica with mythological scenes: No **488:** urn showing the horrific death of Aktaeon, torn apart by his dogs set upon him by Artemis; the same scene is shown on the clay alabaster No **12767.** No **1061, 2317:** Theseus with the Minotaur. No **398, 490:** Peleus fighting with Thetis. No **16350:** Murder of Alkyoneus by Herakles; there is a small Hinged Hypnos (Sleep) on the body of the sleeping giant. No **517:** Herakles wrestling with Kyknos. About 500 B.C.

Show-case 75: Black-figured vases and figurines of the late 6th century, from Attica. No **550:** Achilles being led by his father Peleus to the Centaur Chiron; made around 500 B.C. by the "painter of Edinburgh". No **1045:** oinochoe with symposium theme of the late 6th century B.C. made by Xenokles and painted by Kleisophos, as stated in the inscription: Ξενοκλῆς Κλείσοφος ἐποίησεν: ἔγραψεν (Made, painted, by Xenokles, Kleisophos).

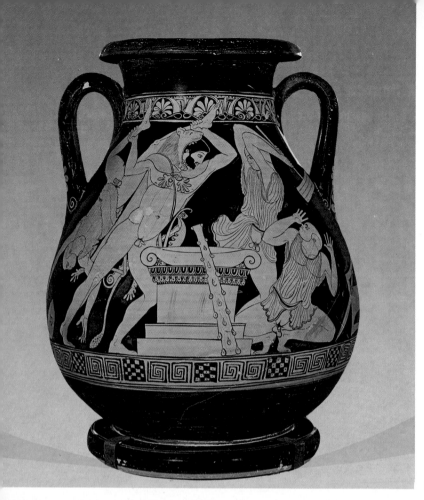

146. Red-figured pelike from Thespiae No 9683 showing Herakles in Egypt fighting against king Boussiris and his men.

147. Fragment of red-figured vase Acr. No 609 with fine representation of a man holding a guitar: a work of the painter Epiktetos.

148. Representation of the red-figured kylix No 1628 showing a young warrior putting on his helmet.

Show-case 66: Black-figured skyphoi, lekythoi, loutrophoroi a.o.: No **12531:** skyphos with fountain, a common theme in black-figured vases. No **402** and **447:** small Panathenian amphorae.

Base No 19312. Panathenian amphora: shown on the front side is Athena turned to the left, between two Doric columns topped by cocks; on the rear side, the chariot race won by the owner of the vase.

Show-case 67: Black-figured pottery (urns, skyphoi, alabasters, plates) of the late 6th century and the early 5th century B.C.: No **2183** and **2184:** ''epinetron'' or ''onos'', a clay utensil women placed on their laps and thighs while spinning wool. No **2239:** black-painted cantharus with the inscription *"Τεισίας ἐποίησεν"* (made by Teisias).

Show-case 68: Vases from graves found near Brauron, at the site of the sanctuary of Artemis: No **19308:** red-figured cylix showing reveller. No **19310:** black-painted pyxis: engraved on the handle of the cap is the inscription ''Euarches'' and on the outside of the bottom, another saying: *"Εὐάρχες εἰμὶ ἔδοκε Χαριτύλος"* (I was given to Euarches by Charitylos).

Show-case 69: Black-figured Attic vases of the late 6th century B.C. No **539:** amphora showing Theseus and the Minotaur. No **564,** hydria with representation of seated figures being Dionysos, Herakles, Athena and Iolaos. The rest of the vessel is black.

Base no 1361. Chalice-like crater from the Acropolis, showing maenad chased by satyr; a belt of anthemions on the upper part, a belt of meander below.

Base No 735: Chalice-like crater from the Acropolis, by the ''painter of Syriskos'', showing the killing of the Minotaur by Theseus: behind Theseus is

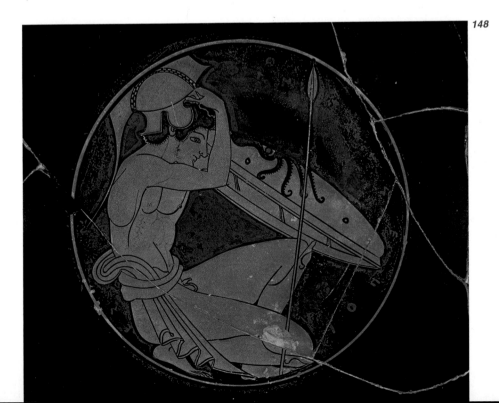

Ariadne and behind her is Minos. On the other side of the vessel, four mythical characters are shown: Orneus, standing; Pallas (seated and looking to the left), Nissos and Lykos. All the names are mentioned in inscriptions.

Show-case 76: Fragments of black-figured and red-figured vases from the Acropolis; they are works by the "painter of Cerberus", Oltos, the "painter of Euergides", Smikros, Euphronios, Epiktetos. Clay tablets with various representations; black-painted oil lamps: No **15125:** fragment of black-figured Attic painting by Paseas; the representation shows Herakles and his nephew Iolaos on a quadriga; beside them is Athena with the characteristic helmet. No **15141;** another work by Paseas: Athena Promachos on a clay board; 510-500 B.C. No **15214:** the National Museum possesses no whole work by the great vase-painter Euphronios; these glued fragments are parts of a cylix dedicated by the painter to Athena on the Acropolis; only part of a representation showing the wedding of Peleus and Thetis is preserved; in the middle, Thetis is being led away by Peleus; in front is the quadriga waiting to take the newly-weds home; deities are standing behind them, the last figure being Athena; the painter's signature has been preserved: *"[Εὐφρό]νιος ἔγραφσεν"* (painted by Euphronios). In spite of the fragmented condition of the vase, one cannot help admiring the perfection of the design, the rendering of the anatomy, the richness in the folds of the garments, the unsurpassed precision of detail. 520-510 B.C.

Show-case 77: Attic vases of the early red-figured period, around 520-490 B.C. No **15002:** white clay alabaster made by the potter Passiadis from Delphi, showing a Maenad and an Amazon. No **1409:** red-figured cylix representing young man with shield. No **1431:** red-figured kylix showing reveller. No **1628:** red-figured cylix by the potter Phindias; pictured on the inside is a naked warrior kneeling while he puts on his helmet with the right hand; in his left hand he holds his shield which is decorated by an octopus with tentacles spread apart; sticking upright to the ground is his spear; the warrior also wears jambs. The form of the composition has been dictated by the circular form of the surface, skilfully utilized by the otherwise unknown painter; running round the edge is the inscription *"Φιντίας ἐποίεσεν"* (made by Phindias). 500 B.C. No **1357:** red-figured cylix with representation of bearded man leaning back on cushions while he sings; his right hand is playing with a rattle, his left is stroking a rabbit; a mat basket is hanging above; coming out of the singer's mouth are the first words of a couplet by the poet Theognis (I. 1365-66):

> "oh thou, most beautiful and most desirable of boys,
> stay and listen to my words"

About 500 B.C.

Base No 450. Black-figured loutrophoros with death scene; around the dead, mourning men and women relatives; late 6th century B.C. No **1452:** red-figured loutrophoros with representation on the same theme.

The loutrophoros was a utensil connected with the wedding ceremonies in Athens: it was used to carry water from the Calliroe fountain for the bride's bath. However the same vase, made of clay or of marble or shown in relief on a stele, was used to mark the graves of unmarried persons, both men and women.

Show-case 70: Red-figured vases and vase fragments from the Acropolis, many of them dedicated to Athena Ergane (patron-goddess of workers) by the craftsmen themselves; they include works by Makron and Hiero, Douris, Brygos, the "painter of Pan", Phindias, Epiktetos ("painter of Kleophrades"). No **609:** fragment of red-figured vase found on the Acropolis with part of a representation of a noble and distinguished looking bearded guitar-player, wearing a wreath on his head; by Epiktetos; 500-490 B.C.

Show-case 71: Red-figured and sculptured vases of the early 5th century: No **1666:** the so-called "cylix of Trikoupis", donated to the National Museum by that eminent Greek politician; shown on the inside, a young man pouring a libation on an altar; on the outside, Herakles fighting with the giant Antaeos, and Theseus with Procrustes; of about 490 B.C. Inside the mouth of the cylix held by the young man, there is the "exclamation": "Oh, Douris". The cylix is twice inscribed with the phrase: "beautiful Athenodotos" also found in other vessels of the same period. No **15375:** red-figured aryballos-like urn signed by Douris as the potter: two Eros-figures are pursuing a youth, and one lashes out at him with a whip. The inscription states: "The urn belongs to Asopodoros". About 480 B.C.

Show-case 72: Corinthian vases and figurines (korae, sirens, gorgons).

Show-case 78: Red-figured Attic urns and other vases with a variety of representations of the period 480-460 B.C.

Base No 18543. Red-figured amphora by the "painter of Syleas" representing the legend of Theseus and the bull of Marathon.

Rooms 55-56. White lekythoi, epinetron from Eretria

White urns: The white urns are an important, separate category of 5th-century Attic pottery. As indicated by their name, these urns were white and after the first decades, they came to be used exclusively for funeral purposes.

These vases with the cylindrical body, the upright, band-like handle, the tall neck and the low disc-shaped base were the receptacles in which aromatic oils were kept.

The technique of white pottery, as seen in the mature works of this room, did not appear all of a sudden; it was preceded by a transitional period represented by many fine examples. In this early period the background of the vase is not white but yellowish or light grey and the figures are drawn in black. The themes are varied, often inspired by mythology or everyday life. In the lekythoi of the mature period, the subject is one: death.

In these white lekythoi the vase is first covered with a white coat and on this white background, the outlines were drawn in black. What distinguishes the new technique is that in addition to the white colour of the background and the black of the outlines, many other colours of striking variety and vividness were used.

As already pointed out, the illustration of white lekythoi were exclusively about death; decoration of the funeral stele; the dead laid out and surrounded by mourning relatives, a dead woman laid to rest by Hypnos and Thanatos, Hermes as the conductor of souls leading the dead to Hades (a scene already seen in Room 16 No 4485); relatives of the deceased visiting the grave with offerings. Not infrequently the deceased is shown sitting on his grave's steps; representations of Charon standing in his boat and waiting to ferry the deceased across the river Acheron, are also common.

White lekythoi have been found almost exclusively in Athenian or Attic graves. A great number was also found in Eretria and in some other places including Cyprus, Naukratis, Sicily and Lower Italy. It is believed that these vases have been taken there by Athenian emigrants.

The most important white vase painter is the so-called "painter of Achilles"; the National Museum possesses a number of his works.

The mature period of white vases covers, approximately, the years from 470 to 460 B.C.; by the end of the 5th century, when they practically stopped being produced, a large number of high quality specimens had accumulated, as this Room demonstrates.

The white lekythoi technique was used to a limited extent with pyxid and cylices. A few white cylices with representations of high artistic value have been preserved. Examples are the partially preserved one showing the murder of Orpheus in this Room (show-case 80, No 15190), the cylix of Kamiros now in the British Museum showing Aphrodite on a swan, and the cylix of Delphi with Apollo offering a libation. White cylices, however, in spite of their superb art never became common because they were luxury articles, fit to be dedicated to the gods, but unsuitable for everyday use.

Show-case 79: White lekythoi of the early period; No **1776:** representation of Night, as a winged woman, clad in a black himation, walking towards the right.

149. White Attic lecythus No 1935 from Eretria, painted by the "painter of Bosanquet"; shown in the middle is the grave with its stele, on the left the dead young hoplite carrying his spear and on the right a relative bringing offerings in a basket.

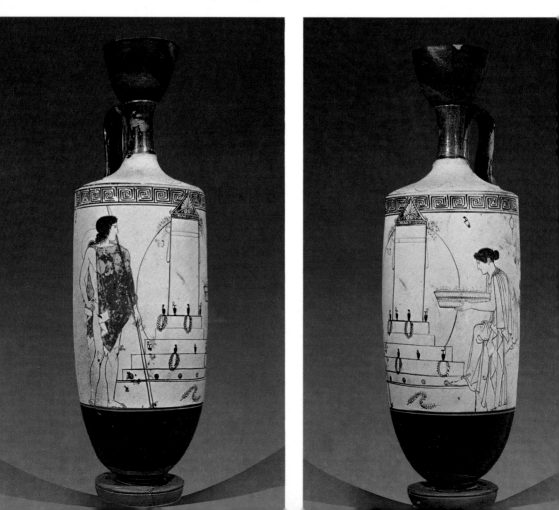

Show-case 88: White and red-figured lekythoi, red-figured vases and figurines: No **16351,** red-figured hydria, showing Hermes as conductor of souls, by the "painter of Syriskos". With the caduceus in his left hand, Hermes holds a bearded dead man with the other, leading him away; 460 B.C. No **1346, 14047, 1788** a.o. are works by the "painter of Icarus". No **17640** is a small red-figured lekythos, painted with Danae, daughter of the king of Argos Akrisios. Because, according to a prophecy Danae was to have a son who would kill Akrisios, the latter kept her imprisoned in an underground guarded room made of copper; but Zeus transformed himself into golden rain and so managed to reach Danae who later gave birth to Perseus. Here Danae, seated on a klismos, is accepting the golden rain of Zeus into her outstreched arms.

Base No 9683. Red-figured pelike from Thespiae. Pictured is an adventure of Herakles in Egypt, where the mythical Egyptian king Bousiris decided to sacrifice him in order to save his country from a famine. Using one of the Egyptians as a cudgel, Herakles overpowers his other assailants; in the middle, fine altar decorated with helices and cymatia on a two-step base; a work of the "painter of Pan", about 470 B.C.

Show-case 80, No 15190: partially preserved white cylix from the Acropolis, picturing the horrible death of Orpheus at the hands of Thracian women; what is preserved of the representation shows, on the left, part of a Thracian woman holding an axe and, on the right, part of Orpheus raising his guitar in an effort to ward off the terrible blow; both figures are majestically serene and of unparalleled beauty, as was indeed the entire art of that period, regardless of its object; there will be passion demonstrated later but not yet. The cylix was painted by the so-called "painter of Pistoxenos" and dates from the decade 470-460 B.C. The potter who made the vase was Euphronios. No **1725, 12806, 2189, 479, 16457:** white-bottomed clay alabasters.

Show-case 81: The "painter of Achilles" is one of the outstanding white lekythoi painters: some of his earlier work, from the period 470-430 B.C. is exhibited in this case.

Show-case 89: White and red-figured lekythoi and red-figured vases; included among the white lekythoi are some by the "painter of Athens 1826", dating from 470-460 B.C.

Show-case 82: Clay reliefs from Melos: No **4196:** Frixos on the ram with the golden fleece, 470-450 B.C. The small red-figured pelike deals with the same subject (No **16023**). No **15878:** Aktaeon, grand-son of Apollo, is killed by his dogs, set upon him by Artemis.

Show-case 83: White lekythoi and red-figured vases: No **1959:** white lekythos with dead man sitting on the steps of the pedestal of his funeral stele, on the right; on the left, woman holding basket. No **1650:** red-figured aryballos-like lekythos with a scene in the women's quarters.

Show-case 84. No 17916: White lekythos with representation of Charon in his ferry; as he waits, Hermes as conductor of souls leads a young woman to him; a work by the "painter of Charon" or "Sabouroff"; about 450 B.C. No **1818**, white lekythos by the "painter of Achilles"; standing in front of a seated woman on the left, a young warrior holds his round shield in his left hand and his helmet in his outstretched right hand; the poignancy of this silent farewell is intensified by the eye decorating the shield; found in Eretria and dating from 450-440 B.C. No **1935**: white lekythos by the "painter of Bosanquet", representing a visit to the grave; in the middle a funeral stele with anthemion on the pediment, and a base of six steps decorated with wreaths and small funeral vases; the mound over the grave is seen at the back; on the left is the dead: a young man with chlamys, spear and a broad-brimmed hat, looks - himself invisible - at a woman relative approaching the grave with offerings - wreaths in a basket; from Eretria, about 440 B.C.

Show-case 90: Marble vases found as offerings in graves, mainly alabasters, marble eggs, pyxides.

Show-case 85: Red-figured vases and white lekythoi; the latter painted by the "painter of Charon" and the "painter of Achilles" with death scenes, visits to graves, Charon, the dead person.

Show-case 86. White lekythoi: No **12783**: Hypnos and Thanatos (Sleep and Death), two winged, bearded men, are conducting a dead woman to the islands of the Makares, imaginary islands in the "western ocean", a place where the souls of the heroes went, a place of bliss for the dead; painted by the "painter of the square" around 420 B.C. No **1926**: white lekythos showing, left, Charon in his ferry, in the middle Hermes with the caduceus in his left hand, and the hat "petassos" on his head, reaching out to take hold of a woman wrapped in a black himation; images of dead people, souls, hovering about; painted by the "painter of Charon", 450-440 B.C.

Show-case 87: Red-figured lekythoi and white lekythoi showing relatives visiting graves, mainly.

Show-case 91: Red-figured vases, white lekythoi and figurines: No **1291**: red-figured pyxis picturing the myth of the three Old Women, sisters of the Gorgons; their names were Enno, Pemphredo and Deino and they had between them one tooth and one eye which they took turns using and which were stolen by Perseus. 430-420 B.C.

Show-case 92: Red figured vases, pelikes, lekythoi. Six white (**19353-19358**) and four black-figured (**19359-19362**) vases were funeral offerings found in a marble sarcophagus in Anabyssos in 1960. No **19353** is by the "painter of Achilles". The representation on lekythos No **19355** is unusual: a woman lamenting with excessive passion before a mound with a loutrophoros on top.

Show-case 95: White lekythoi and red-figured vessels. No **1489**: cauldron showing the hunt of the Caledonian Boar, by the "painter of Akragas", about 450 B.C.

Base No 17918. Red-figured hydria by the "painter of Peleus" showing interior of a room with music-playing women.

Base No 18063. Red-figured jar (*stamnos*) by the vase painter Polygnotos, showing Theseus abducting Helen with the help of his friend Peirithous; the names of the personages are indicated by inscriptions: Theseus with Helen, Peirithous climbing on chariot, and Phoibe.

Show-case 93, No **1172**: wedding cauldron with wedding scene on rounded part; pictured on the lower part are Apollo, Artemis, Leto and Hermes; about 470 B.C. No **1240**: loutrophoros with wedding scene. No **1250**: wedding cauldron with scene in women's quarters.

Show-case 96: Red-figured vases: hydriae, pelikes, oinochoae, craters, pyxides, epinetrons; No **1167:** crater with scene from satyric drama: Prometheus with the fire in a narthex and dancing satyrs; by the "painter of Orpheus". No **1467:** red-figured pelike by the "painter of Kassel", showing Apollo and two Muses. About 420 B.C.

Show-case 94: White lekythoi from a sarcophagus found at Anabyssos, and red-figured vases.

Show-case 97: White lekythoi and red-figured vases. No **2028:** Charon on the shore of Acheron, facing a dead young woman, by the "painter of reed", late 5th century B.C. No **19280:** fragment of white lekythos with two women whose postures seem to express acceptance of the inevitability of death; the importance of the hands, expressing as it were, the feelings of the persons, has been pointed out.

Show-case 98: Red-figured choae with Dionysiac scenes or scenes connected with children. "Choae" were oinochoae of clover-shape and were so called after the name of the second day of the *Anthesteria*, which was the great festival of Dionysos in Athens; young children went to the festival carrying small vases of this kind painted with scenes of children's lives. Many choae with relative scenes were found as kterismata in children's graves. Adults used these vases at the festival of Dionysos as wine jugs and the scenes on them were related to wine-drinking; e.g. No **1218** pictures a drunken Dionysos being supported by a bald drunken satyr; following behind them is a little satyr holding a choe. About 430 B.C.

On the wall - No 3935: Funeral stele of Pyraechme, an old woman shown seated and holding a skyphos, with a large choa at her feet; this may be symbolic of her death or of her occupation as a nanny; the latter information is provided by the inscription: "Pyraechme, a good nanny". About 380 B.C.

Show-case 99: Attic white lekythoi: No **1816:** this is one of the best known Attic white lekythoi: the deceased, a young warrior, is sitting on the steps of the base of the grave holding his spears; on his right, a young man on the left is addressing the girl. The dead man does not show the serene unconcern that had characterized the earlier lekythoi; his face seems brooding - which is certainly not unrelated to the period when the vase was painted. About 410 B.C.

Show-case No 101: Black-painted vases, oinochoae, cantharus, skyphoi, feeding-bottles, pyxides, kyathoi. No **18588:** Rhyton in the shape of a duck's head.

Show-case 103, No 1629: Epinetron from Eretria, by the "painter of Eretria": in the foreground, a goddess in relief, nearby Peleus and Thetis; Thetis transforms herself in order to avoid Peleus, whom she will marry eventually. On one side is Alkestis leaning on her nuptial bed and watching her girl-friends who are decorating two wedding cauldrons and a loutrophoros; two others are playing with a pigeon. The scene depicted on the other side is from the marriage of Harmonia and includes her mother Aphrodite, Imeros, Eros and Hebe. About 425 B.C. No **15308:** red-figured choa with fragment of a symposium scene; a crowned young man is lying on a bed; holding an empty cylix in his right hand, he watches a harp-playing hetaera; painted by the "painter of Eretria" at the same time as the epinetron.

Show-case 104: Red-figured vases, canthari, small lekythoi, pelikes etc. No **14501:** pelike painted with scene of sacrifice. No **15882,** same type of vase, showing farewell scene. No **19367:** figurine of Aphrodite, holding a pigeon, about 430 B.C. No **13605:** clay figurine of a female acrobat. No **1631:** oinochoe with two javelin-throwing horsemen.

Show-case 102: Nos **1681, 1253, 1171:** three red-figured wedding cauldrons.

Show-case 105. Wedding cauldrons: No **14790-14791:** scenes in the women's quarters by the "painter of the bath". About 420 B.C.

Base No 1333. Red-figured pelike with representation of battle between gods and giants; among the foremost figures are the Dioscuri and Ares fighting against four giants - a composition inspired by a then famous painting. About 400 B.C.

Show-case 108: No **1388:** Red-figured crater with wedding scene by the "painter of the Athens wedding", end of the 5th century B.C. No **13027:** dinos with representation of flute-player and dancers of satyric drama.

Show-case 106: Sculptured vases: No **2059:** Group of two figures on rectangular base; winged male figure, possibly Thanatos (Death), supports woman who seems about to collapse. No **2060:** fine bust of nude Aphrodite emerging from the waves out of an open shell; around her neck, a rich necklace set off with golden paint.

Show-case 107: Black-figured and white lekythoi, red-figured vases (donated by G. Empedokles).

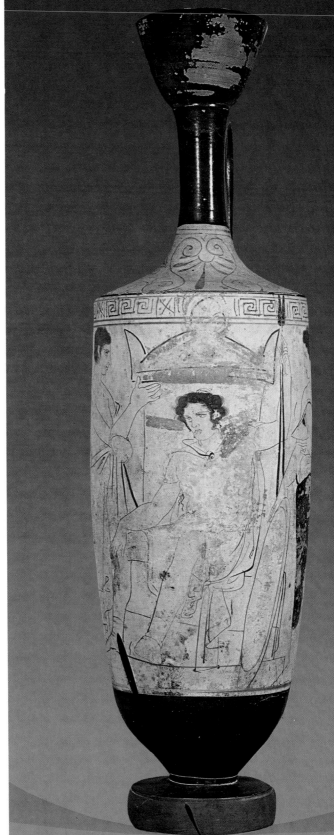

150. White Attic lecythus No 1927 with representation of Haron in the boat with which he ferries the dead across lake Acherousia. On the shore of the lake on the left, a young woman awaits the ferry.

151. Famous Attic lecythus No 1816 from Eretria; in front of the adorned stele of his grave, the dead man is sitting with a thoughtful expression, holding his spears; to the left, a young woman is carrying the dead man's shield and helmet while a young man to the right seems to be speaking to the woman.

152. Young athlete from the representation of the Panathenian amphora No 20044.

Panathenian amphorae: The so-called Panathenian amphorae form a particular class of black-figured vases. The Panathenian amphorae, filled with oil from the sacred olive-trees (the "moreae") of Attica, were given as prizes to the victors of the Panathenian Games held in Athens every four years.

The earliest Panathenian amphorae date from the time of Klitias, the painter of the vase known as "François", about 570 B.C., and the last are of the 2nd century B.C. Their representations accord with a strictly defined tradition: Pictured on one side of the vase was the goddess Athena, standing in war-like attire with aegis, shield, helmet and spear, turning left, between two columns topped with a cock each. Beside, and parallel to, the left column, there is the inscription ·"τῶν Ἀθήνηθεν ἄθλων" (a prize from the Games at Athens). The shield of Athena is always set with a coat-of-arms which varies from one painter to another.

In three amphorae - one in the British Museum and the two others in Hildsheim, Germany - the coat-of-arms shown on Athena's shield consists of a representation of the bronze statues of the "Tyrant-Killers" Armodios and Aristogeiton, made by the sculptors Kritios and Nessiotis and erected in Athens in 476 B.C. This is believed to be a reference to the overthrow of the Thirty Tyrants and to the restoration of democracy in Athens, in the autumn of 403 B.C. These amphorae were given as prizes at the games held in the summer of 402 B.C.

The rear side of the vase is always painted with a scene connected with the particular competition won by the victor: hoplite race, stadium race, wrestling, boxing, pentathlon, chariot race.

The style of the representations on the Panathenian amphorae changes very gradually, while the technique (black-figured) remains unchanged. Some of the changes, associated mainly with the composition of the representations, are of interest because they are helpful in dating the amphorae. From the beginning of the 4th century B.C., it becomes customary to inscribe the amphorae with the name of the ruling archon of Athens in whose year of office the oil given as a prize was produced. At about the same time, the cocks standing on top of the columns flanking Athena begin to be replaced by other symbols, including likenesses of existing statues in Athens. The amphorae of 360/59 B.C. show on the columns the popular sculptural group of Irene (Peace) holding the infant Plutos (Wealth) in her arms, a work of the sculptor Kephisodotos, father of the great Praxiteles.

From 363/2 B.C., Athena's shield, including of course the coat-of arms, is shown in side view. In 360/59, the goddess who always used to look to the left, now turns around and looks to the right, which results in the shield showing the inner side; as a consequence, the coat of arms disappears.

Many Panathenian amphorae have been preserved, intact or in fragments. Most were found in graves, where they had accompanied their dead owners or in sanctuaries to which they had been dedicated by the winners.

Table: Nos 20044 - 20049: Six Panathenian amphorae of the 4th century B.C. found in fragments in storage areas by the side of a busy ancient road in Eretria. They show the Athena scene on one side, and a scene connected with wrestling or pankration i.e. the competitions at which the unknown winners had excelled, on the other; they also show the traditional inscription "A prize from the Games at Athens", and the name of archon: Charikleides (363/62 B.C.) and Kallimedes (360/59 B.C.)

Show-case 120: Vases and figurines from the sanctuary of Kavira in Boeotia, showing the characteristic silhouetting technique. In one partly preserved vase, there is the inscription "Σμίκρος ἀνέθεκε Καβίροι" (dedicated to Kaviri by Smikron). No **424:** skyphos with humoristic representation of wedding procession; the newly married couple are in the carriage. Late 5th early 4th century B.C.

Show-case 119: Red-figured and black-figured vases and figurines from Boeotian workshops. Worthy of note is the red-figured chalice-like crater representing a cock-fight watched by two Eroses, one standing and one kneeling. Late 5th century B.C.

Show-case 118: Black-painted, red-figured and black-coated vases found at Vourvoura of Kynouria (Arcadia); works of local artists.

Show-case 109: Large red-figured craters, showing mostly Dionysiac scenes; late 5th to early 4th century B.C.

Show-case 110: Red-figured vases and clay figurines. No **17297:** hydria with representation of deities connected with the Eleusinian Mysteries: Demeter sitting on a rock, Persephone, Herakles, Iakhos. No **4692:** clay figurine of woman from Tanagra, a specimen of the celebrated figurines of that town; about 330 B.C.

153. Red-figured pelike No 1718 of the so-called Kerts style, showing gifts being offered to a newly wed couple.

Show-case 117: Corinthian red-figured vases. No **12260:** a scene in the women's quarters. No **537:** plate showing Persephone on throne. No **4160:** clay figurine of Aphrodite with Eros on her side, of the first half of the 4th century B.C. No **4164:** Aphrodite figurine of the latter half of the 4th century B.C.; the nude goddess is emerging from an open shell.

Show-case 111: Red-figured vases, mainly craters, and clay figurines. No **12490:** chalice-like crater showing Dionysos, Ariadne, Eroses, satyrs and maenads; in the middle are Dionysos and Ariadne (the daughter of Minos whom Dionysos had married) surrounded by white-painted winged Eroses; the rest of the vase is taken up by the retinue of Dionysos. Early 4th century B.C.

Show-case 112, No **1472:** red-figured pelike with bathing women; in the middle, a naked woman, kneeling, is washing her hair, while another woman standing to the right, is pouring water from a hydria over her head. About 330 B.C.

Show-case 116: Red-figured, chalice-like craters.

Show-case 115, No **12544:** red-figured chalice-like crater with a scene including a young woman weighing something on scales. Eros and Anteros, the sons of Ares and Aphrodite; a young man is beside the woman; a work of the "painter of Erotostasia", about 330 B.C. No **12545:** similar crater picturing the Judgment of Paris by the same painter.

Show-case 113, No **1718:** red-figured pelike of the Kerts style, from about 330 B.C., showing "epaulia" i.e. the gifts customarily sent by friends and relatives to a married couple on the second day after the wedding; the colours used - white, golden and blue - are significant. No **11037:** large red-figured skyphos; on the mouth, votive inscription in molded golden characters. No **1635:** Attic red-figured pyxis, three-legged, showing Leto leaning against a palm-tree in Delos, about to give birth to Apollo, the most beautiful of the gods. Then, in the words of the poet Theognis: *"πᾶσα μὲν ἐπλήσθη Δῆλος ἀπειρεσίη ὀδμῆς ἀμβροσίης, ἐγέλασε δὲ γαῖα πελώρη, γήθησεν δὲ βαθὺς πόντος ἁλὸς πολιῆς"* (The whole, Delos was filled with ambrosia smell, the wide Earth laughed, and the deep, salty sea sounded).

The colours included in the painting are white, blue, green and golden, the latter colour dominating the representation of the palm-tree. About 340-330 B.C.

Show-case 114: Mainly large red-figured craters. No **1181:** red-figured pelike showing the "Judgment of Paris"; dressed in his oriental garb, Paris, in the presence of Hermes, is surrounded by Athena, Hera and Aphrodite, among whom he is to choose the most beautiful - no easy task for the royal prince, if one is to judge by his thoughtful expression; painted by the "painter of Marcyas", 340-330 B.C.

On the wall. No **11036:** red-figured clay plaque, an offering according to the inscription shown below, of Ninnios to Demeter and Persephone - "the only document that can be conclusively connected with the Eleusinian cult" (G. Mylonas). It is temple-shaped with a pediment and a central acroterium decorated with an anthemion. The three representations shown have been variously interpreted. G. Mylonas believes that the main representation in the upper belt shows a preliminary ceremony of the Minor Eleusinian Mysteries, and the lower belt a ceremony of the Major Mysteries; in both scenes, initiates present themselves to Demeter; the presence of Iakhos in the lower picture indicates that the procession is approaching its terminal in Eleusis. Second half of the 4th century B.C.

154. *The famous red-figured epinetron No 1629 from Eretria; in front, bust of a goddess in relief; on the right side, Alcestis and her three girl friends are decorating a marital cauldron and a loutrophoros; two others are playing with a dove.*

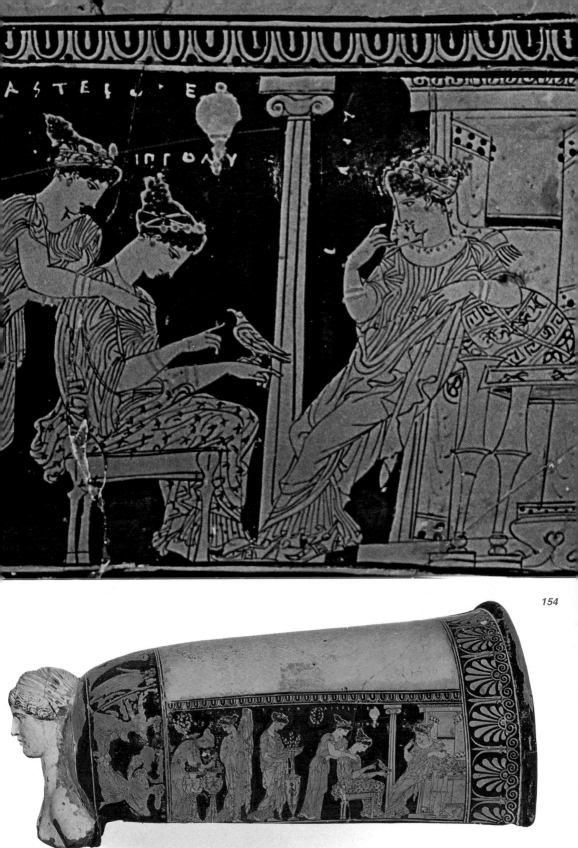

154

Room 48, of Thera

The discovery of the prehistoric city at Akrotiri in Thera and the excavations begun in 1967 have been among the most important archaeological events of the 20th century. The city was destroyed around 1500 B.C. by a tremendous explosion of the island's volcano; excavated, much of the city was found in an excellent state of preservation: intact frescoes, utensils in their proper places, streets, etc.

The island's civilization was typically Cycladic and though it had received influences from the Minoan civilization, it had not lost all of its own characteristic features.

The show-cases in this room contain vases found at the excavation of Akrotiri, some of them made locally, others imported. Of particular interest among the multitude of vases and utensils is prochoe No **928** in show-case **1**: the reddish ears of barley on a uniform pale background are simply and realistically painted. Noteworthy in show-case **2**, which contains locally-made pottery, are the variously decorated boat-shaped vases (*kymves*): one is painted with three lilies, another has black dolphins leaping over brown waves, still another flying swallows, the messengers of spring. The clay rhyton painted with a bull in show-case **4** was used for ceremonial purposes; the animal's body is covered with woolen net, which has religious significance. Interesting in show-case **7** is the clay rhyton in the shape of a lion-head with pronounced features; it is a copy of a gold or silver vessel like those seen in the Mycenaean collection.

The frescoes of Thera: By far the most important finds of the excavation of Akrotiri are the frescoes ornamenting the houses of the prehistoric city. While the vases and the other objects found provide valuable information about life in pre-historic Thera, the frescoes are direct, almost photographic, evidence of what that ancient people and its activities were like; some, e.g. the fisherman or the boxing scene, are pictures of everyday life, others, like the "house of the ladies", give details of dress, and some even tell a whole story, like the fresco of the "nautical expedition".

155. *Mural painting from Thera showing two antelope: on the light background, the animals are painted with dark contours while red is used only in the head to outline the necessary details.*

156. *Clay prochus from Thera with multi-coloured representation of water birds; they are still flying but just about to touch the earth as shown by their extended legs; broad red and brown bands surround the scene.*

157. *Beaker from Thera with flying swallow.*

158. *Mural painting from Thera with two young children boxing; the figure on the left wears boxing gloves and is adorned with jewels, earrings, a necklace etc.; the only garment is a loin-cloth.*

159. *Mural painting from Thera: a naked fisherman holds a bunch of fish in each hand.*

160. *Large fresco known as the "nautical campaign"; miniature ships with their crews and passengers, dolphins swimming around, houses with their inhabitants, wild beasts hunting others, mountains, trees, are depicted with realism, motion and originality. Possibly, the composition represents the narration of a tale.*

161. *Miniature mural painting from Thera showing a tropical landscape; trees, palms, birds and wild animals, all in vividly depicted motion, are shown around a river.*

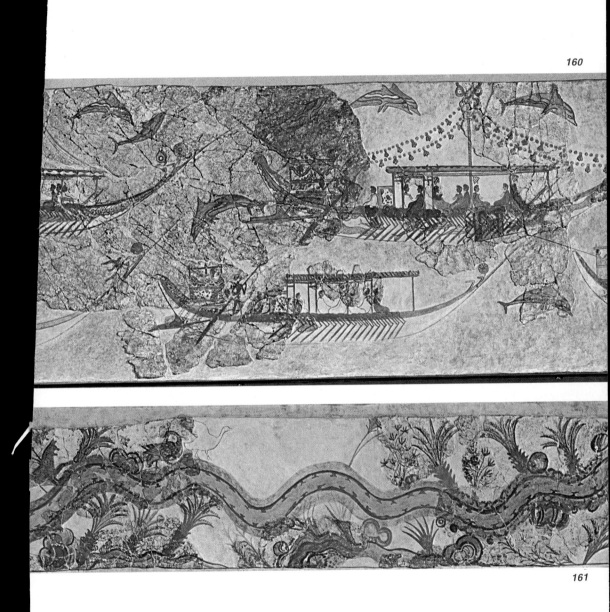